CPCU 540 Course Guide

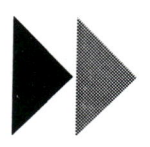

Finance for Risk Management
and Insurance Professionals
3rd Edition

The Institutes
720 Providence Road, Suite 100
Malvern, Pennsylvania 19355-3433

© 2009
American Institute For Chartered Property Casualty Underwriters

All rights reserved. This book or any part thereof may not be reproduced without the written permission of the copyright holder.

Unless otherwise apparent, examples used in The Institutes materials related to this course are based on hypothetical situations and are for educational purposes only. The characters, persons, products, services, and organizations described in these examples are fictional. Any similarity or resemblance to any other character, person, product, services, or organization is merely coincidental. The Institutes are not responsible for such coincidental or accidental resemblances.

This material may contain Internet Web site links external to The Institutes. The Institutes neither approve nor endorse any information, products, or services to which any external Web sites refer. Nor do The Institutes control these Web sites' content or the procedures for Web site content development.

The Institutes specifically disclaim any implied warranties of merchantability or fitness for a particular purpose. No warranty may be created or extended by sales representatives or written sales materials.

The Institutes materials related to this course are provided with the understanding that The Institutes are not engaged in rendering legal, accounting, or other professional service. Nor are The Institutes explicitly or implicitly stating that any of the processes, procedures, or policies described in the materials are the only appropriate ones to use. The advice and strategies contained herein may not be suitable for every situation.

3rd Edition • 4th Printing • July 2010

ISBN 978-0-89463-394-2

Contents

Study Materials..iii
Student Resources..iv
Using This Course Guide...iv
About the CPCU 540 Exam..vi
CPCU 540 Key Formulas...viii
Present and Future Value Tables Provided on Exam..x
CPCU Advisory Committee...xiv

Assignments

1. Basics of Corporate Finance..1.1
2. Financial Statements...2.1
3. Sources of Additional Financial and Nonfinancial Information...3.1
4. Financial Statement Analysis...4.1
5. Working Capital Management...5.1
6. Time Value of Money..6.1
7. Discounted Cash Flow Valuation...7.1
8. Bonds and Stocks...8.1
9. Operating Environment and Corporate Finance...9.1
10. Insurer Investment Strategies..10.1
11. Insurer Income and Dividend Policy...11.1
12. Insurer Capital: Needs and Sources...12.1
13. Capital Structure of Insurers..13.1
14. Making Capital Investment Decisions..14.1
15. Mergers and Acquisitions...15.1

Exam Information..1
Canons and Rules of the CPCU Code of Professional Ethics...5

Study Materials Available for CPCU 540

James M. Olsen, *Finance for Risk Management and Insurance Professionals*, 1st ed., 2006, AICPCU/IIA.
CPCU 540 *Course Guide*, 3rd ed., 2009, AICPCU/IIA (includes access code for SMART Online Practice Exams).
CPCU 540 SMART Study Aids—Review Notes and Flash Cards, 2nd ed.
Introduction to Accounting Principles and Financial Statements (DVD).

Student Resources

Catalog A complete listing of our offerings can be found in *Succeed*, the Institutes' professional development catalog, including information about:

- Current programs and courses
- Current textbooks, course guides, SMART Study Aids, and online offerings
- Program completion requirements
- Exam registration

To obtain a copy of the catalog, visit our Web site at www.TheInstitutes.org or contact Customer Service at (800) 644-2101.

How to Prepare for Institute Exams This free handbook is designed to help you by:

- Giving you ideas on how to use textbooks and course guides as effective learning tools
- Providing steps for answering exam questions effectively
- Recommending exam-day strategies

The handbook is printable from the Student Services Center on the Institutes' Web site at www.TheInstitutes.org, or available by calling Customer Service at (800) 644-2101.

Educational Counseling Services To ensure that you take courses matching both your needs and your skills, you can obtain free counseling from the Institutes by:

- E-mailing your questions to advising@TheInstitutes.org
- Calling an Institutes' counselor directly at (610) 644-2100, ext. 7601
- Obtaining and completing a self-inventory form, available on our Web site at www.TheInstitutes.org or by contacting Customer Service at (800) 644-2101

Exam Registration Information As you proceed with your studies, be sure to arrange for your exam.

- Visit our Web site at www.TheInstitutes.org forms to access and print the Registration Booklet, which contains information and forms needed to register for your exam.
- Plan to register with the Institutes well in advance of your exam.

How to Contact the Institutes For more information on any of these publications and services:

- Visit our Web site at www.TheInstitutes.org
- Call us at (800) 644-2101 or (610) 644-2100 outside the U.S.
- E-mail us at customerservice@TheInstitutes.org
- Fax us at (610) 640-9576
- Write to us at The Institutes, Customer Service, 720 Providence Road, Suite 100, Malvern, PA 19355-3433

Using This Course Guide

This course guide will help you learn the course content and prepare for the exam.

Each assignment in this course guide typically includes the following components:

Educational Objectives These are the most important study tools in the course guide. Because all of the questions on the exam are based on the Educational Objectives, the best way to study for the exam is to focus on these objectives.

Each Educational Objective typically begins with one of the following action words, which indicate the level of understanding required for the exam:

Analyze—Determine the nature and the relationship of the parts.

Apply—Put to use for a practical purpose.

Associate—Bring together into relationship.

Calculate—Determine numeric values by mathematical process.

Classify—Arrange or organize according to class or category.

Compare—Show similarities and differences.

Contrast—Show only differences.

Define—Give a clear, concise meaning.

Describe—Represent or give an account.

Determine—Settle or decide.

Evaluate—Determine the value or merit.

Explain—Relate the importance or application.

Identify or list—Name or make a list.

Illustrate—Give an example.

Justify—Show to be right or reasonable.

Paraphrase—Restate in your own words.

Recommend—Suggest or endorse something to be used

Summarize—Concisely state the main points.

Required Reading The items listed in this section indicate the study materials that correspond to the assignment.

Outline The outline lists the topics in the assignment. Read the outline before the required reading to become familiar with the assignment content and the relationships of topics.

Key Words and Phrases These words and phrases are fundamental to understanding the assignment and have a common meaning for those working in insurance. After completing the required reading, test your understanding of the assignment's Key Words and Phrases by writing their definitions.

Review Questions The review questions test your understanding of what you have read. Review the Educational Objectives and required reading, then answer the questions to the best of your ability. When you are finished, check the answers at the end of the assignment to evaluate your comprehension.

Application Questions These questions continue to test your knowledge of the required reading by applying what you've studied to "hypothetical" real-life situations. Again, check the suggested answers at the end of the assignment to review your progress.

Sample Exam Your course guide includes a sample exam (located at the back) or a code for accessing SMART Online Practice Exams (which appears on the inside back cover). Use the option available for the course you're taking to become familiar with the test format.

For courses that offer SMART Online Practice Exams, you can either download and print a sample credentialing exam or take full practice exams using questions like those that will appear on your credentialing exam. SMART Online Practice Exams are as close as you can get to experiencing an actual exam before taking one.

More Study Aids

The Institutes also produce supplemental study tools, called SMART Study Aids, for many of our courses. When SMART Study Aids are available for a course, they are listed on both page iii of this course guide and on the first page of each assignment. SMART Study Aids include Review Notes and Flash Cards and are excellent tools to help you learn and retain the information in each assignment.

About the CPCU 540 Exam

The CPCU 540 exam contains more financially oriented content than our other CPCU exams. Therefore, you will have access to more financial information resources during the exam, as explained in these frequently asked questions:

Q: What resources are available on the computer on which I am taking the exam?

A: During the exam, a drop-down menu offers access to key financial formulas as well as present value and future value tables.

Q: Which financial formulas are provided on the exam and which formulas do I need to memorize?

A: A list of the formulas provided in the exam is included in the front of this course guide. The exam provides only the formulas on this list. You must memorize all other necessary formulas. A sample list of formulas NOT provided on the exam is also included in the front of this course guide.

Q: Which present and future value tables are included on the exam?

A: An abbreviated version of the present and future value tables that appear in the textbook (*Finance for Risk Management and Insurance Professionals*, 1st ed.) are included in the exam, such as these:

- • Future value of $1 at the end of *n* periods (Exhibit 6-1, page 6.7)
- • Present value of $1 to be received after *n* periods (Exhibit 6-4, page 6.13)
- • Future value of an annuity of $1 per period for *n* periods (Exhibit 7-2, page 7.6)
- • Present value of an annuity of $1 per period for *n* periods (Exhibit 7-4, page 7.9)

The tables on the exam do not cover as many periods or as many different interest rates as the tables in the textbook but do provide all of the values needed to answer exam questions.

Q: Can I use a financial calculator while taking the exam?

A: Although a financial calculator is not required for the exam, you are allowed to use any solar or battery powered calculator other than one with alphabetic keys or paper tape. A calculator that permits the input of alphabetic keys (a, b,..., y, z) for the formation of words is not permitted. Any business/financial calculators, including those that are programmable, that meet these criteria are permitted. A financial calculator will not be provided by the testing center.

Q. Can I use a PDA or cell phone as a calculator?

A. No, the only electronic device allowed during an exam is a calculator as described in the question above.

Q: To answer questions that ask for present or future value, do I need to use the formula to calculate the present value or future value factors or can I use the tables that are provided?

A: There are three different methods you can use to earn full credit for an answer to a present or future value question on the exam:

1. Use a financial calculator to determine the correct answer.

2. Use the present or future value tables provided in the exam reference materials to obtain the present value or future value factors used to calculate the answer.

3. Use the formulas provided to calculate the answer.

Two fast ways to calculate answers are using the tables and using a financial calculator.

Q: Is there a recommended method for calculating present or future value problems?

A: No, there is no recommended method. All three methods (tables, calculator, and formula) are acceptable methods for calculating the answer on the exam. Where applicable, the solutions provided to the problems in the course guide show all three methods of calculating the correct answers.

Q: Which calculator was used to determine the solutions shown in the course guide?

A: The Texas Instruments BA II Plus was used to determine the solutions shown in the course guide. However, the course guide does not provide complete information on how to use this or any other financial calculator. To ensure that you are using your calculator's financial functions properly, consult the calculator's user guide.

Q: Are there any common financial calculator mistakes that students often make?

A: Yes, there are some common mistakes that students make when trying to solve CPCU 540 exam problems with a financial calculator, including these two:

1. *Trying to learn how to use a financial calculator during the CPCU 540 exam*—If you plan on using a financial calculator during the exam, ensure that you know how to use it properly beforehand. You will not be allowed to consult your calculator's user guide during the exam.

2. *Not resetting values*—Most financial calculators store the values entered for present value and future value calculations in their memory. Students who fail to reset these values before each calculation on the exam may find that their incorrect answers are based on values from previous calculations.

CPCU 540 Key Formulas

Students will be expected to be able to respond to each of the educational objectives of the course. The following listings are meant as a study aid, not a replacement of the educational objectives.

Formulas Provided at National Exam

The following formulas and tables will be provided in a drop-down menu format during the national exam. Students will be expected to apply them, given appropriate data.

Future Value Over Multiple Periods (Chapter 6)

$$FV = PV \times (1 + r)^n,$$

where FV = future value at the end of n periods, PV = present value or value at the beginning of the period, r = interest rate, and n = number of periods.

Future Value Over Multiple Periods With Payment Periods Less Than One Year (Chapter 6)

$$FV = PV \times (1 + (r \div m))^{n \times m},$$

where m = number of times per year interest is paid.

Effective Interest Rate (Chapter 6)

$$EAR = (1 + (r \div m))^m - 1.$$

Present Value (Chapter 6)

$$PV = FV \div (1 + r)^n.$$

Future Value of an Ordinary Annuity (Chapter 7)

$$FVA = A \times [((1 + r)^n - 1) \div r],$$

where A = amount of periodic payment.

Future Value of an Annuity Due (Chapter 7)

$$FVA \text{ due} = FVA \times (1 + r).$$

Present Value of an Ordinary Annuity (Chapter 7)

$$PVA = A \times [(1 - (1 \div (1 + r)^n)) \div r].$$

Present Value of an Annuity Due (Chapter 7)

$$PVA \text{ due} = PVA \times (1 + r).$$

Present Value of a Perpetuity (Chapter 7)

$$PVP = A \div r.$$

Future Value of a Stream of Unequal Payments (Chapter 7)

$$FV_s = (C_1 \times (1 + r)^{n-1}) + (C_2 \times (1 + r)^{n-2}) + \ldots + (C_n \times (1 + r)^{n-t}),$$

where C_t = payment at end of year t and t = year in which payment is made.

Present Value of a Stream of Unequal Payments (Chapter 7)

$$PV_s = (C_1 \div (1 + r)^t) + (C_2 \div (1 + r)^t) + (C_3 \div (1 + r)^t) + \ldots + (C_n \div (1 + r)^n).$$

The Fisher Effect (Chapter 8)

$$1 + \text{Nominal rate of return} = (1 + \text{Real rate of return}) \times (1 + \text{Inflation rate}).$$

The Value of a Bond (Chapter 8)

$$B = (C \div (1 + i)) + (C \div (1 + i)^2) + \ldots + (C \div (1 + i)^n) + (F \div (1 + i)^n),$$

where B = bond value, C = coupon of the bond in time period t, i = discount rate, F = face value of the bond, and n = years to maturity.

The Dividend Growth Model (Chapter 8)

$$V_0 = D_1 \div (r - g),$$

where V_0 = value at time 0 (current), D_1 = dividends per share at time 1 (the end of next period), r = market rate of return required for this investment, and g = annual constant percentage growth in dividends per share.

Value of dividend at time t: $D_t = D_0 \times (1 + g)^t$.

Capital Asset Pricing Model (CAPM) (Chapter 10)

$$R_p = r_f + \beta_p (r_m - r_f),$$

where R_p = expected rate of return on portfolio, r_f = risk-free rate of return, and β_p = portfolio's beta.

Insurer's Total Income (Chapter 11)

$$TI = UG + NII + RCG + UCG + OI,$$

where TI = total income, UG = underwriting gain, NII = net investment income, RCG = realized capital gains and losses, UCG = unrealized capital gains and losses, and OI = other income.

After-Tax Cost of Debt (Chapter 13)

$$\text{After-tax cost of debt} = i \times (1 - T),$$

where T = marginal tax rate.

Net Present Value (Chapter 14)

$$NPV = -C_0 + (C_1 \div (1 + r)^t) + (C_2 \div (1 + r)^t) + \ldots + (C_n \div (1 + r)^n).$$

Internal Rate of Return (Chapter 14)

$$0 = -C_0 + (C_1 \div (1 + r)^t) + (C_2 \div (1 + r)^t) + (C_3 \div (1 + r)^t) + \ldots + (C_n \div (1 + r)^n).$$

Present and Future Value Tables

Selected FV, PV, FVA, and PVA factor tables

Sample of Formulas Not Provided at Exam

Students will be expected to know the following equations and be able to apply them, given appropriate data.

The Accounting Equation (Chapter 2)

Assets = Liabilities + Owners' equity.

The Net Income Equation (Chapter 2)

Net income = Revenue − Expenses − Income taxes.

Net Profit Margin (Chapter 4)

Net profit margin = Net income ÷ Sales.

Return on Assets (ROA) (Chapter 4)

Return on assets (ROA) = Net income ÷ Total assets.

Return on Equity (ROE) (Chapter 4)

Return on equity (ROE) = Net income ÷ Owners' equity.

Asset Turnover (Chapter 4)

Asset turnover = Sales ÷ Total assets.

Equity Multiplier (Chapter 4)

Equity multiplier = Total assets ÷ Owners' equity.

DuPont Identity (Chapter 4)

DuPont identity = (Net profit margin) × (Total asset turnover) × (Equity multiplier).

Combined Ratio (Chapter 4)

Combined ratio = Loss ratio + Expense ratio.

Loss Ratio (Chapter 4)

Loss ratio = (Losses + LAE) ÷ Earned premiums.

Financial Basis Expense Ratio (Chapter 4)

Financial basis expense ratio = Underwriting expenses ÷ Earned premiums.

Trade Basis Expense Ratio (Chapter 4)

Trade basis expense ratio = Underwriting expenses ÷ Written premiums.

Investment Yield Ratio (Chapter 4)

Investment yield ratio = Net investment earnings ÷ Invested assets.

Return on Policyholders' Surplus (Chapter 4)

Return on policyholders' surplus = Net income ÷ Policyholders' surplus.

Accounts Receivable Turnover Ratio (Chapter 4)

Accounts receivable turnover ratio = Credit sales ÷ Accounts receivable.

Days Sales Outstanding (Chapter 4)

Days sales outstanding = 365 ÷ Accounts receivable turnover ratio.

Inventory Turnover Ratio (Chapter 4)

Inventory turnover ratio = Cost of goods sold ÷ Inventory.

Working Capital (Chapter 4)

Working capital = Current assets − Current liabilities.

Current Ratio (Chapter 4)

Current ratio = Current assets ÷ Current liabilities.

Acid-Test Ratio, or Quick Ratio (Chapter 4)

Acid-test ratio = (Cash + Marketable securities + Accounts receivable) ÷ Current liabilities.

Liquidity Ratio (Chapter 4)

Liquidity ratio = (Cash + Invested assets) ÷ (Unearned premium reserve + Loss and LAE reserve).

Debt-to-Equity Ratio (Chapter 4)

Debt-to-equity ratio = Long-term debt ÷ Owners' equity.

Debt-to-Assets Ratio, or Debt Ratio (Chapter 4)

Debt-to-assets ratio = Total liabilities ÷ Total assets.

Premium-to-Surplus Ratio (Chapter 4)

Premium-to-surplus ratio = Net written premiums ÷ Policyholders' surplus.

Reserves-to-Surplus Ratio (Chapter 4)

Reserves-to-surplus ratio = (Unearned premium reserve + Loss and LAE reserve) ÷ Policyholders' surplus.

Dividend Yield (Chapter 10)

Dividend yield = Dividend ÷ Share price at start of year.

Percentage Capital Gain (Chapter 10)

Percentage capital gain = Capital gain ÷ Share price at start of year.

Percentage Total Return (Chapter 10)

Percentage total return = (Capital gain + Dividend) ÷ Share price at start of year.

Market Risk Premium (Chapter 10)

Market risk premium = Expected market return − Risk-free return.

Note: Use of a financial calculator is not required for this course; however, it is recommended. Non-programmable financial calculators can be used during the national exam. Acceptable calculators include the HP 10b and the TI Business Analyst II. Financial calculators will not be provided by the testing centers.

Future Value of $1 at the End of n Periods = $(1 + i)^n$

Interest Rate

Period	1%	2%	3%	4%	5%	6%	7%	8%	9%	10%	12%	14%	16%	18%	20%
1	1.0100	1.0200	1.0300	1.0400	1.0500	1.0600	1.0700	1.0800	1.0900	1.1000	1.1200	1.1400	1.1600	1.1800	1.2000
2	1.0201	1.0404	1.0609	1.0816	1.1025	1.1236	1.1449	1.1664	1.1881	1.2100	1.2544	1.2996	1.3456	1.3924	1.4400
3	1.0303	1.0612	1.0927	1.1249	1.1576	1.1910	1.2250	1.2597	1.2950	1.3310	1.4049	1.4815	1.5609	1.6430	1.7280
4	1.0406	1.0824	1.1255	1.1699	1.2155	1.2625	1.3108	1.3605	1.4116	1.4641	1.5735	1.6890	1.8106	1.9388	2.0736
5	1.0510	1.1041	1.1593	1.2167	1.2763	1.3382	1.4026	1.4693	1.5386	1.6105	1.7623	1.9254	2.1003	2.2878	2.4883
6	1.0615	1.1262	1.1941	1.2653	1.3401	1.4185	1.5007	1.5869	1.6771	1.7716	1.9738	2.1950	2.4364	2.6996	2.9860
7	1.0721	1.1487	1.2299	1.3159	1.4071	1.5036	1.6058	1.7138	1.8280	1.9487	2.2107	2.5023	2.8262	3.1855	3.5832
8	1.0829	1.1717	1.2668	1.3686	1.4775	1.5938	1.7182	1.8509	1.9926	2.1436	2.4760	2.8526	3.2784	3.7589	4.2998
9	1.0937	1.1951	1.3048	1.4233	1.5513	1.6895	1.8385	1.9990	2.1719	2.3579	2.7731	3.2519	3.8030	4.4355	5.1598
10	1.1046	1.2190	1.3439	1.4802	1.6289	1.7908	1.9672	2.1589	2.3674	2.5937	3.1058	3.7072	4.4114	5.2338	6.1917
11	1.1157	1.2434	1.3842	1.5395	1.7103	1.8983	2.1049	2.3316	2.5804	2.8531	3.4785	4.2262	5.1173	6.1759	7.4301
12	1.1268	1.2682	1.4258	1.6010	1.7959	2.0122	2.2522	2.5182	2.8127	3.1384	3.8960	4.8179	5.9360	7.2876	8.9161
13	1.1381	1.2936	1.4685	1.6651	1.8856	2.1329	2.4098	2.7196	3.0658	3.4523	4.3635	5.4924	6.8858	8.5994	10.6993
14	1.1495	1.3195	1.5126	1.7317	1.9799	2.2609	2.5785	2.9372	3.3417	3.7975	4.8871	6.2613	7.9875	10.1472	12.8392
15	1.1610	1.3459	1.5580	1.8009	2.0789	2.3966	2.7590	3.1722	3.6425	4.1772	5.4736	7.1379	9.2655	11.9737	15.4070
16	1.1726	1.3728	1.6047	1.8730	2.1829	2.5404	2.9522	3.4259	3.9703	4.5950	6.1304	8.1372	10.7480	14.1290	18.4884
17	1.1843	1.4002	1.6528	1.9479	2.2920	2.6928	3.1588	3.7000	4.3276	5.0545	6.8660	9.2765	12.4677	16.6722	22.1861
18	1.1961	1.4282	1.7024	2.0258	2.4066	2.8543	3.3799	3.9960	4.7171	5.5599	7.6900	10.5752	14.4625	19.6733	26.6233
19	1.2081	1.4568	1.7535	2.1068	2.5270	3.0256	3.6165	4.3157	5.1417	6.1159	8.6128	12.0557	16.7765	23.2144	31.9480
20	1.2202	1.4859	1.8061	2.1911	2.6533	3.2071	3.8697	4.6610	5.6044	6.7275	9.6463	13.7435	19.4608	27.3930	38.3376
25	1.2824	1.6406	2.0938	2.6658	3.3864	4.2919	5.4274	6.8485	8.6231	10.8347	17.0001	26.4619	40.8742	62.6686	95.3962
30	1.3478	1.8114	2.4273	3.2434	4.3219	5.7435	7.6123	10.0627	13.2677	17.4494	29.9599	50.9502	85.8499	143.3706	237.3763
35	1.4166	1.9999	2.8139	3.9461	5.5160	7.6861	10.6766	14.7853	20.4140	28.1024	52.7996	98.1002	180.3141	327.9973	590.6682
40	1.4889	2.2080	3.2620	4.8010	7.0400	10.2857	14.9745	21.7245	31.4094	45.2593	93.0510	188.8835	378.7212	750.3783	1469.772
50	1.6446	2.6916	4.3839	7.1067	11.4674	18.4202	29.4570	46.9016	74.3575	117.3909	289.0022	700.2330	1670.704	3927.357	9100.438

Present Value of $1 to Be Received After n Periods = $1 \div (1 + r)^n$

Interest Rate

Period	1%	2%	3%	4%	5%	6%	7%	8%	9%	10%	12%	14%	16%	18%	20%
1	0.9901	0.9804	0.9709	0.9615	0.9524	0.9434	0.9346	0.9259	0.9174	0.9091	0.8929	0.8772	0.8621	0.8475	0.8333
2	0.9803	0.9612	0.9426	0.9246	0.9070	0.8900	0.8734	0.8573	0.8417	0.8264	0.7972	0.7695	0.7432	0.7182	0.6944
3	0.9706	0.9423	0.9151	0.8890	0.8638	0.8396	0.8163	0.7938	0.7722	0.7513	0.7118	0.6750	0.6407	0.6086	0.5787
4	0.9610	0.9238	0.8885	0.8548	0.8227	0.7921	0.7629	0.7350	0.7084	0.6830	0.6355	0.5921	0.5523	0.5158	0.4823
5	0.9515	0.9057	0.8626	0.8219	0.7835	0.7473	0.7130	0.6806	0.6499	0.6209	0.5674	0.5194	0.4761	0.4371	0.4019
6	0.9420	0.8880	0.8375	0.7903	0.7462	0.7050	0.6663	0.6302	0.5963	0.5645	0.5066	0.4556	0.4104	0.3704	0.3349
7	0.9327	0.8706	0.8131	0.7599	0.7107	0.6651	0.6227	0.5835	0.5470	0.5132	0.4523	0.3996	0.3538	0.3139	0.2791
8	0.9235	0.8535	0.7894	0.7307	0.6768	0.6274	0.5820	0.5403	0.5019	0.4665	0.4039	0.3506	0.3050	0.2660	0.2326
9	0.9143	0.8368	0.7664	0.7026	0.6446	0.5919	0.5439	0.5002	0.4604	0.4241	0.3606	0.3075	0.2630	0.2255	0.1938
10	0.9053	0.8203	0.7441	0.6756	0.6139	0.5584	0.5083	0.4632	0.4224	0.3855	0.3220	0.2697	0.2267	0.1911	0.1615
11	0.8963	0.8043	0.7224	0.6496	0.5847	0.5268	0.4751	0.4289	0.3875	0.3505	0.2875	0.2366	0.1954	0.1619	0.1346
12	0.8874	0.7885	0.7014	0.6246	0.5568	0.4970	0.4440	0.3971	0.3555	0.3186	0.2567	0.2076	0.1685	0.1372	0.1122
13	0.8787	0.7730	0.6810	0.6006	0.5303	0.4688	0.4150	0.3677	0.3262	0.2897	0.2292	0.1821	0.1452	0.1163	0.0935
14	0.8700	0.7579	0.6611	0.5775	0.5051	0.4423	0.3878	0.3405	0.2992	0.2633	0.2046	0.1597	0.1252	0.0985	0.0779
15	0.8613	0.7430	0.6419	0.5553	0.4810	0.4173	0.3624	0.3152	0.2745	0.2394	0.1827	0.1401	0.1079	0.0835	0.0649
16	0.8528	0.7284	0.6232	0.5339	0.4581	0.3936	0.3387	0.2919	0.2519	0.2176	0.1631	0.1229	0.0930	0.0708	0.0541
17	0.8444	0.7142	0.6050	0.5134	0.4363	0.3714	0.3166	0.2703	0.2311	0.1978	0.1456	0.1078	0.0802	0.0600	0.0451
18	0.8360	0.7002	0.5874	0.4936	0.4155	0.3503	0.2959	0.2502	0.2120	0.1799	0.1300	0.0946	0.0691	0.0508	0.0376
19	0.8277	0.6864	0.5703	0.4746	0.3957	0.3305	0.2765	0.2317	0.1945	0.1635	0.1161	0.0829	0.0596	0.0431	0.0313
20	0.8195	0.6730	0.5537	0.4564	0.3769	0.3118	0.2584	0.2145	0.1784	0.1486	0.1037	0.0728	0.0514	0.0365	0.0261
25	0.7798	0.6095	0.4776	0.3751	0.2953	0.2330	0.1842	0.1460	0.1160	0.0923	0.0588	0.0378	0.0245	0.0160	0.0105
30	0.7419	0.5521	0.4120	0.3083	0.2314	0.1741	0.1314	0.0994	0.0754	0.0573	0.0334	0.0196	0.0116	0.0070	0.0042
35	0.7059	0.5000	0.3554	0.2534	0.1813	0.1301	0.0937	0.0676	0.0490	0.0356	0.0189	0.0102	0.0055	0.0030	0.0017
40	0.6717	0.4529	0.3066	0.2083	0.1420	0.0972	0.0668	0.0460	0.0318	0.0221	0.0107	0.0053	0.0026	0.0013	0.0007
50	0.6080	0.3715	0.2281	0.1407	0.0872	0.0543	0.0339	0.0213	0.0134	0.0085	0.0035	0.0014	0.0006	0.0003	0.0001

Future Value of an Annuity of $1 Per Period for n Periods = $[(1 + r)^n - 1] \div r$

Interest Rate

Period	1%	2%	3%	4%	5%	6%	7%	8%	9%	10%	12%	14%	16%	18%	20%
1	1.0000	1.0000	1.0000	1.0000	1.0000	1.0000	1.0000	1.0000	1.0000	1.0000	1.0000	1.0000	1.0000	1.0000	1.0000
2	2.0100	2.0200	2.0300	2.0400	2.0500	2.0600	2.0700	2.0800	2.0900	2.1000	2.1200	2.1400	2.1600	2.1800	2.2000
3	3.0301	3.0604	3.0909	3.1216	3.1525	3.1836	3.2149	3.2464	3.2781	3.3100	3.3744	3.4396	3.5056	3.5724	3.6400
4	4.0604	4.1216	4.1836	4.2465	4.3101	4.3746	4.4399	4.5061	4.5731	4.6410	4.7793	4.9211	5.0665	5.2154	5.3680
5	5.1010	5.2040	5.3091	5.4163	5.5256	5.6371	5.7507	5.8666	5.9847	6.1051	6.3528	6.6101	6.8771	7.1542	7.4416
6	6.1520	6.3081	6.4684	6.6330	6.8019	6.9753	7.1533	7.3359	7.5233	7.7156	8.1152	8.5355	8.9775	9.4420	9.9299
7	7.2135	7.4343	7.6625	7.8983	8.1420	8.3938	8.6540	8.9228	9.2004	9.4872	10.0890	10.7305	11.4139	12.1415	12.9159
8	8.2857	8.5830	8.8923	9.2142	9.5491	9.8975	10.2598	10.6366	11.0285	11.4359	12.2997	13.2328	14.2401	15.3270	16.4991
9	9.3685	9.7546	10.1591	10.5828	11.0266	11.4913	11.9780	12.4876	13.0210	13.5795	14.7757	16.0853	17.5185	19.0859	20.7989
10	10.4622	10.9497	11.4639	12.0061	12.5779	13.1808	13.8164	14.4866	15.1929	15.9374	17.5487	19.3373	21.3215	23.5213	25.9587
11	11.5668	12.1687	12.8078	13.4864	14.2068	14.9716	15.7836	16.6455	17.5603	18.5312	20.6546	23.0445	25.7329	28.7551	32.1504
12	12.6825	13.4121	14.1920	15.0258	15.9171	16.8699	17.8885	18.9771	20.1407	21.3843	24.1331	27.2707	30.8502	34.9311	39.5805
13	13.8093	14.6803	15.6178	16.6268	17.7130	18.8821	20.1406	21.4953	22.9534	24.5227	28.0291	32.0887	36.7862	42.2187	48.4966
14	14.9474	15.9739	17.0863	18.2919	19.5986	21.0151	22.5505	24.2149	26.0192	27.9750	32.3926	37.5811	43.6720	50.8180	59.1959
15	16.0969	17.2934	18.5989	20.0236	21.5786	23.2760	25.1290	27.1521	29.3609	31.7725	37.2797	43.8424	51.6595	60.9653	72.0351
16	17.2579	18.6393	20.1569	21.8245	23.6575	25.6725	27.8881	30.3243	33.0034	35.9497	42.7533	50.9804	60.9250	72.9390	87.4421
17	18.4304	20.0121	21.7616	23.6975	25.8404	28.2129	30.8402	33.7502	36.9737	40.5447	48.8837	59.1176	71.6730	87.0680	105.9306
18	19.6147	21.4123	23.4144	25.6454	28.1324	30.9057	33.9990	37.4502	41.3013	45.5992	55.7497	68.3941	84.1407	103.7403	128.1167
19	20.8109	22.8406	25.1169	27.6712	30.5390	33.7600	37.3790	41.4463	46.0185	51.1591	63.4397	78.9692	98.6032	123.4135	154.7400
20	22.0190	24.2974	26.8704	29.7781	33.0660	36.7856	40.9955	45.7620	51.1601	57.2750	72.0524	91.0249	115.3797	146.6280	186.6880
25	28.2432	32.0303	36.4593	41.6459	47.7271	54.8645	63.2490	73.1059	84.7009	98.3471	133.3339	181.8708	249.2140	342.6035	471.9811
30	34.7849	40.5681	47.5754	56.0849	66.4388	79.0582	94.4608	113.2832	136.3075	164.4940	241.3327	356.7868	530.3117	790.9480	1181.8816
35	41.6603	49.9945	60.4621	73.6522	90.3203	111.4348	138.2369	172.3168	215.7108	271.0244	431.6635	693.5727	1120.7130	1816.6516	2948.3411
40	48.8864	60.4020	75.4013	95.0255	120.7998	154.7620	199.6351	259.0565	337.8824	442.5926	767.0914	1342.0251	2360.7572	4163.2130	7343.8578
50	64.4632	84.5794	112.7969	152.6671	209.3480	290.3359	406.5289	573.7702	815.0836	1163.909	2400.018	4994.521	10435.649	21813.094	45497.191

Present Value of an Annuity of $1 Per Period for n Periods = [1 − (1 ÷ (1 + r)^n)] ÷ r

Interest Rate

Period	1%	2%	3%	4%	5%	6%	7%	8%	9%	10%	12%	14%	16%	18%	20%
1	0.9901	0.9804	0.9709	0.9615	0.9524	0.9434	0.9346	0.9259	0.9174	0.9091	0.8929	0.8772	0.8621	0.8475	0.8333
2	1.9704	1.9416	1.9135	1.8861	1.8594	1.8334	1.8080	1.7833	1.7591	1.7355	1.6901	1.6467	1.6052	1.5656	1.5278
3	2.9410	2.8839	2.8286	2.7751	2.7232	2.6730	2.6243	2.5771	2.5313	2.4869	2.4018	2.3216	2.2459	2.1743	2.1065
4	3.9020	3.8077	3.7171	3.6299	3.5460	3.4651	3.3872	3.3121	3.2397	3.1699	3.0373	2.9137	2.7982	2.6901	2.5887
5	4.8534	4.7135	4.5797	4.4518	4.3295	4.2124	4.1002	3.9927	3.8897	3.7908	3.6048	3.4331	3.2743	3.1272	2.9906
6	5.7955	5.6014	5.4172	5.2421	5.0757	4.9173	4.7665	4.6229	4.4859	4.3553	4.1114	3.8887	3.6847	3.4976	3.3255
7	6.7282	6.4720	6.2303	6.0021	5.7864	5.5824	5.3893	5.2064	5.0330	4.8684	4.5638	4.2883	4.0386	3.8115	3.6046
8	7.6517	7.3255	7.0197	6.7327	6.4632	6.2098	5.9713	5.7466	5.5348	5.3349	4.9676	4.6389	4.3436	4.0776	3.8372
9	8.5660	8.1622	7.7861	7.4353	7.1078	6.8017	6.5152	6.2469	5.9952	5.7590	5.3282	4.9464	4.6065	4.3030	4.0310
10	9.4713	8.9826	8.5302	8.1109	7.7217	7.3601	7.0236	6.7101	6.4177	6.1446	5.6502	5.2161	4.8332	4.4941	4.1925
11	10.3676	9.7868	9.2526	8.7605	8.3064	7.8869	7.4987	7.1390	6.8052	6.4951	5.9377	5.4527	5.0286	4.6560	4.3271
12	11.2551	10.5753	9.9540	9.3851	8.8633	8.3838	7.9427	7.5361	7.1607	6.8137	6.1944	5.6603	5.1971	4.7932	4.4392
13	12.1337	11.3484	10.6350	9.9856	9.3936	8.8527	8.3577	7.9038	7.4869	7.1034	6.4235	5.8424	5.3423	4.9095	4.5327
14	13.0037	12.1062	11.2961	10.5631	9.8986	9.2950	8.7455	8.2442	7.7862	7.3667	6.6282	6.0021	5.4675	5.0081	4.6106
15	13.8651	12.8493	11.9379	11.1184	10.3797	9.7122	9.1079	8.5595	8.0607	7.6061	6.8109	6.1422	5.5755	5.0916	4.6755
16	14.7179	13.5777	12.5611	11.6523	10.8378	10.1059	9.4466	8.8514	8.3126	7.8237	6.9740	6.2651	5.6685	5.1624	4.7296
17	15.5623	14.2919	13.1661	12.1657	11.2741	10.4773	9.7632	9.1216	8.5436	8.0216	7.1196	6.3729	5.7487	5.2223	4.7746
18	16.3983	14.9920	13.7535	12.6593	11.6896	10.8276	10.0591	9.3719	8.7556	8.2014	7.2497	6.4674	5.8178	5.2732	4.8122
19	17.2260	15.6785	14.3238	13.1339	12.0853	11.1581	10.3356	9.6036	8.9501	8.3649	7.3658	6.5504	5.8775	5.3162	4.8435
20	18.0456	16.3514	14.8775	13.5903	12.4622	11.4699	10.5940	9.8181	9.1285	8.5136	7.4694	6.6231	5.9288	5.3527	4.8696
25	22.0232	19.5235	17.4131	15.6221	14.0939	12.7834	11.6536	10.6748	9.8226	9.0770	7.8431	6.8729	6.0971	5.4669	4.9476
30	25.8077	22.3965	19.6004	17.2920	15.3725	13.7648	12.4090	11.2578	10.2737	9.4269	8.0552	7.0027	6.1772	5.5168	4.9789
35	29.4086	24.9986	21.4872	18.6646	16.3742	14.4982	12.9477	11.6546	10.5668	9.6442	8.1755	7.0700	6.2153	5.5386	4.9915
40	32.8347	27.3555	23.1148	19.7928	17.1591	15.0463	13.3317	11.9246	10.7574	9.7791	8.2438	7.1050	6.2335	5.5482	4.9966
50	39.1961	31.4236	25.7298	21.4822	18.2559	15.7619	13.8007	12.2335	10.9617	9.9148	8.3045	7.1327	6.2463	5.5541	4.9995

CPCU Advisory Committee

F. Scott Addis, CPCU
The Addis Group

Chris Amrhein, AAI
Amrhein and Associates, Inc.

Scott A. Behrent, CPCU, AIC
Farm Family Casualty Insurance Company

Mark J. Browne, PhD
University of Wisconsin, Madison School of Business

Anne Crabbs, CPCU
State Auto Insurance Companies

Richard A. Derrig
OPAL Consulting

Eric A. Fitzgerald
Marshall, Dennehey, Warner, Coleman & Goggin

Joseph A. Gerber, Esq.
Cozen O'Connor

Dennis M. Halligan, CPCU
Farmers Group

Joseph S. Harrington, CPCU, ARP
American Association of Insurance Services

Frederick P. Hessenthaler, CPCU
Chubb & Son

Steven M. Horner, CPCU, CLU, AIM, ARM
Horner & Associates, LLC

Robert E. Hoyt, PhD, CLU, ChFC
University of Georgia

James Jones, CPCU, AIC, ARM, AIS
Katie School of Insurance & Financial Services

John J. Kelly, CPCU, CLU, ChFC, ARM
CPCU Society

Johannah Lipscher, CPCU, AIS
Zurich North America

Stanley L. Lipshultz, Esq., CPCU
Lipshultz & Hone Chartered & Interrisk Ltd.

Dennis F. Mahoney, CEBS, CFP
The Wharton School, University of Pennsylvania

Gregory Massey, CPCU, CIC, CRM, ARM
Selective Insurance Company of America

Michael McVey, CPCU, ARe
Penn National Insurance

Ronald M. Metcho, CPCU, ARM, AAI
Saul-Metcho Insurance

Robin K. Olson, CPCU
International Risk Management Institute, Inc.

Jesus Pedre, CPCU, AIC, AIS
Texas Department of Insurance

Brian P. Savko, CPCU
State Farm Insurance Companies

Wade E. Sheeler, CPCU
Grinnell Mutual Group

James A. Sherlock, CPCU, CLU, ARM
ACE, USA

Angela K. Sparks, CPCU
State Farm Insurance Companies

Christine A. Sullivan, CPCU, AIM
Allstate Insurance Company

Lawton Swan, CPCU, CLU, ARM, CSP, CMC
Interisk Corporation

Sean S. Sweeney, CPCU, RPLU, ARe
Phildelphia Insurance Company

Kenneth J. Swymer, Sr., EdD, CPCU
Liberty Mutual Group

Angela Viane, CPCU, AIS
Zurich North America

Andrew Zagrzejewski, CPCU, AIC
Farmers Group—Los Angeles Service Center

Direct Your Learning

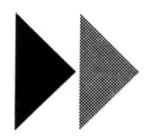

ASSIGNMENT 1

Basics of Corporate Finance

Educational Objectives

After learning the content of this assignment, you should be able to:

1. Describe the following legal forms of business organization and the advantages and disadvantages of each:
   - Sole proprietorships
   - Partnerships
   - Corporations

2. Describe the following goals of corporate finance:
   - Maximization of shareholder wealth
   - Financial transparency
   - Ethical conduct

3. Explain how corporate finance departments are organized and the following activities they perform:
   - Working capital management
   - Capital structure
   - Capital budgeting
   - Accounting

4. Describe the role of financial markets in corporate finance.

5. Contrast primary and secondary financial markets.

Study Materials

Required Reading:
- Finance for Risk Management and Insurance Professionals
  - Chapter 1

Study Aids:
- SMART Online Practice Exams
- SMART Study Aids
  - Review Notes and Flash Cards—Assignment 1

Outline

▶ **Legal Forms of Business Organization**
  A. Sole Proprietorships
      1. Advantages of Sole Proprietorships
      2. Disadvantages of Sole Proprietorships
  B. Partnerships
      1. Advantages of Partnerships
      2. Disadvantages of Partnerships
  C. Corporations
      1. Advantages of Corporations
      2. Disadvantages of Corporations

▶ **Goals of Corporate Finance**
  A. Maximization of Shareholder Wealth
  B. Financial Transparency
  C. Ethical Conduct

▶ **Corporate Finance Departments**
  A. Organization
  B. Key Activities of Corporate Finance Departments
      1. Working Capital Management
      2. Capital Structure
      3. Capital Budgeting
      4. Accounting

▶ **Financial Markets**
  A. Role in Corporate Finance
  B. Primary Markets
  C. Secondary Markets

▶ **Summary**

---

s.m.a.r.t. tips: Don't spend time on material you have already mastered. The SMART Review Notes are organized by the Educational Objectives found in each course guide assignment to help you track your study.

Key Words and Phrases

Define or describe each of the words and phrases listed below.

Finance (p. 1.3)

Corporate finance (p. 1.3)

Sole proprietorship (p. 1.4)

Unlimited liability (p. 1.6)

Partnership (p. 1.6)

General partnership (p. 1.6)

Limited partnership (p. 1.6)

Corporation (p. 1.7)

Board of directors (p. 1.8)

Professional corporation (p. 1.8)

Limited liability company (LLC) (p. 1.9)

Stakeholder (p. 1.11)

Working capital (p. 1.14)

Capital structure (p. 1.15)

Capital budgeting (p. 1.16)

Financial market (p. 1.17)

Securities (p. 1.17)

Money market (p. 1.17)

Capital market (p. 1.17)

Primary market (p. 1.18)

Bid price (p. 1.20)

Asked price (p. 1.20)

Bid-asked spread (p. 1.20)

Secondary markets (p. 1.20)

Market depth (p. 1.21)

Market breadth (p. 1.21)

Review Questions

1. Describe how the following insurance professionals use finance and corporate finance concepts.
    a. Risk management professionals (p. 1.3)

b. Agents and brokers (p. 1.3)

c. Underwriters (p. 1.3)

d. Actuaries (p. 1.3)

e. Claim representatives (p. 1.3)

2. List three general forms of business organization. (p. 1.4)

3. Identify the primary advantages of the following types of business organization:
   a. Sole proprietorships (pp. 1.4–1.5)

   b. Partnerships (pp. 1.6–1.7)

   c. Corporations (p. 1.9)

4. Identify disadvantages of the following types of business organization:
   a. Sole proprietorships (p. 1.6)

   b. Partnerships (p. 1.7)

   c. Corporations (p. 1.9)

5. Distinguish between the business operations of a general partnership and the business operations of a limited partnership. (p. 1.6)

6. Identify the main goals of corporate finance. (p. 1.10)

7. Identify problems that can result from focusing on an overall financial goal of maximizing profits. (p. 1.11)

8. Explain why a board of directors needs financial transparency to ensure shareholders that management is acting in the company's best interests. (p. 1.11)

9. Describe the purpose and the main provisions of the Sarbanes-Oxley Act of 2002 regarding financial reporting of U.S. corporations. (p. 1.12)

10. List several questions that help determine whether a business decision or action is ethical. (p. 1.13)

11. Identify the typical responsibilities of the following corporate financial staff:

   a. Chief financial officer (CFO) (p. 1.14)

   b. Treasurer (p. 1.14)

   c. Controller (p. 1.14)

   d. Chief information officer (CIO) (p. 1.14)

12. Describe the key activities performed by a corporate finance department. (pp. 1.14–1.16)

13. Describe working capital and its components. (p. 1.14)

14. Identify two questions that help a financial manager make decisions regarding resources needed to meet the corporation's long-term goals. (p. 1.15)

15. Describe the components of financial markets. (p. 1.17)

16. Identify the goals of the typical providers and users of capital in financial markets. (p. 1.17)

17. Identify the typical forms of demand for capital in financial markets. (p. 1.18)

18. Identify the primary sources of the supply of capital in financial markets. (p. 1.18)

19. Distinguish between primary and secondary markets. (pp. 1.18–1.20)

20. Identify four types of primary-market structures. (pp. 1.18–1.19)

21. Describe how trading on an organized exchange differs from trading in over-the-counter (OTC) dealer markets. (p. 1.21)

Application Questions

1. Mary Davis has an idea for a business that she can start and operate with a small initial financial investment. Mary believes that within two years the business will need significant additional capital to grow. What form of business organization should Mary consider, and why?

2. When reviewing the financial statements of an insured as part of the renewal process, an underwriter notices that the insured's net income has improved from the prior year; however, the amount spent on repairs and maintenance has decreased substantially from historical levels. In this instance, do you believe the increase in net income reflects an increase in the owners' wealth, and why?

3. Property-casualty insurers do not invest their capital as heavily in fixed assets and equipment as manufacturers. Therefore, why is an insurer's corporate finance department concerned with capital budgeting?

4. If the primary financial markets are the markets in which companies sell their securities to investors to raise capital, why are companies concerned with having secondary markets that function well?

Answers to Assignment 1 Questions

NOTE: These answers are provided to give students a basic understanding of acceptable types of responses. They often are not the only valid answers and are not intended to provide an exhaustive response to the questions.

Review Questions

1. Insurance professionals use finance and corporate finance concepts in the following ways:
   a. Risk management professionals—To determine the most appropriate method of controlling and financing loss exposures
   b. Agents and brokers—To determine whether the organization meets an insurer's overall financial underwriting guidelines and to prepare the insurance application
   c. Underwriters—To decide whether to offer coverage
   d. Actuaries—To develop premium rates
   e. Claim representatives—For claim investigations into the cause of loss

2. The following are three general forms of business organization:
   (1) Sole proprietorship
   (2) Partnership
   (3) Corporation

3. Advantages of the following forms of business organization include:
   a. Sole proprietorship:
      - Owner has full control of the business
      - Profits are taxed once
      - Easy to establish
      - Limited capital requirements
      - Minimal state and federal control
   b. Partnerships:
      - Each partner's share of profits is taxed as personal income
      - Easy to establish
      - Access to several partners' skill sets
      - Shared management responsibilities
      - Access to capital through the combined wealth of the partners
      - Partners' liability is limited to their investment in the partnership
   c. Corporations
      - Shareholders have limited liability for the corporation's debts.
      - Ownership interests can be acquired and transferred easily.
      - Unlimited life since they exist independently of their owners.
      - Greater ability to raise capital.

4. Disadvantages of the following forms of business organization include:
   a. Sole proprietorship
      - Unlimited liability
      - Difficult to raise additional capital
      - Life of business is limited to owner's lifetime
   b. Partnerships:
      - Each individual partner has unlimited liability for all partnership debts
      - Limited existence
      - Shared management can lead to conflict
      - Can be difficult to raise capital
   c. Corporations:
      - Complex and expensive to establish and maintain
      - Corporate income can be subject to double taxation

5. Partners in a general partnership are active in the management and operation of the business, and each partner assumes unlimited liability for all partnership debts. Partners in a limited partnership are legally prohibited from participating actively in the management of the business, and each partner's liability is limited to the amount of capital he or she contributed.

6. The main goals of corporate finance are to maximize shareholder wealth, to provide for transparency in financial reporting, and to conduct financial operations in an ethical manner.

7. Problems that can result from a business's focusing on an overall financial goal of maximizing profits include the following:
   - Focusing on current profits to the detriment of long-term profitability and growth
   - Not accounting for the levels of risk associated with different profit scenarios
   - Electing accounting treatments that make financial statements less useful to potential investors

8. A board of directors needs financial transparency to ensure shareholders that management is acting in the company's best interests. To perform this duty, the board needs access to timely, understandable, informative, and accurate financial reporting that contains full disclosure of key events and accounting methods.

9. The purpose of the Sarbanes-Oxley Act of 2002 is to protect investors by improving the accuracy and reliability of corporate disclosures. The major provisions include:
   - Creation of an oversight board to regulate public accounting firms that audit publicly traded corporations
   - Enhanced financial disclosure requirements
   - Increases in penalties for corporate fraud
   - New requirements for certifying the accuracy of financial information

10. The following questions help determine whether a business decision or action is ethical:
    - Does my decision fall within the guidance of the corporation's code of ethics?
    - Am I willing to have my decision and reasoning reported on the front page of the newspaper?
    - Will the people with whom I have significant personal relationships approve of my decision?

11. Typical responsibilities of the following corporate financial staff include:
    a. Chief financial officer (CFO)—Setting the overall corporate financial strategy
    b. Treasurer—Working capital management, capital structure management, and capital budgeting
    c. Controller—Accounting functions, taxes, and financial reporting
    d. Chief information officer (CIO)—The corporation's information technology

12. The following key activities are performed by a corporate finance department:
    - Working capital management—Focuses on a corporation's short-term needs for cash and other resources
    - Capital structure—Focuses on what resources the corporation needs to meet its long-term goals and how the resources should be obtained
    - Capital budgeting—Planning and managing a corporation's long-term investments
    - Accounting—Accumulating and reporting financial data for both internal and external use

13. Working capital of a corporation is its current assets minus its current liabilities. Current assets include cash, accounts receivable, marketable securities, and inventory. Current liabilities include amounts owed to suppliers and employees, and the current portion of any loans payable.

14. The following two questions help a financial manager make decisions regarding resources needed to meet the corporation's long-term goals:
    - How much capital will be financed by borrowing and how much raised through the sale of stock?
    - What specific financial vehicles will be used to raise capital?

15. Financial markets consist of the following components:
    - Money markets—Markets in which short-term securities are traded.
    - Capital markets—Markets in which long-term securities are traded.

16. The providers of capital in financial markets, as investors, want to find a way to use their money to generate income. The goal of typical users of capital is to find the additional capital needed to finance their business operations.

17. The typical forms of demand for capital in the financial markets include mortgages; corporate and foreign bonds; common and preferred stock; short-term business borrowing; consumer credit, bank loans, other loans, and advances; federal, foreign, state, and local government debt.

18. The primary sources of capital in financial markets are individual investors, insurers, pension funds, thrift institutions, investment companies, commercial banks, and business corporations.

19. Primary markets are used to sell new securities, with the proceeds going straight to the issuer. Secondary markets provide a mechanism for investors to buy and sell previously issued securities.

20. Primary-market structures include the following:
    (1) Direct search—Buyers and sellers rely on word-of-mouth communication of their trading interest to attract trading partners.
    (2) Broker—Finds trading partners and negotiates transaction prices for clients in return for a fee.
    (3) Dealer—Dealers buy for, and sell for, their own accounts at quoted prices.
    (4) Auction—Investors participate in a single price-setting process.

21. Trading on an organized exchange differs from trading in over-the-counter (OTC) dealer markets in the following ways:
    - All trading in a given stock occurs at a single price on an exchange floor.
    - Transaction prices are broadcast to the public.

Application Questions

1. Mary should consider a sole proprietorship. The sole proprietorship is easy and inexpensive to set up. Although the sole proprietorship form of ownership is not effective for raising additional capital, the business could be incorporated in two years when Mary anticipates needing additional capital. If the need for additional capital does not arise at that time, Mary can continue to operate as a sole proprietor.

2. Although the reduction of expenses can increase the company's net income in the short term, not performing repairs and maintenance on the company's equipment can reduce the efficiency of the equipment and shorten its useful life. Both of these results are likely to be more expensive to correct in the long term than making current expenditures to repair and maintain the equipment. Therefore, this short-term increase in net income is not likely to increase the owners' wealth in the long term.

3. Although property-casualty insurers do not invest as heavily in fixed assets and equipment as manufacturers, capital budgeting is still an important function of the corporate finance department of an insurer. The insurance policies sold by the insurer require that a portion of the insurer's capital is available to pay claims and expenses in excess of the premiums received for the policy. Therefore, the decision regarding the types and amounts of insurance to write are capital budgeting decisions.

4. Companies are concerned with having secondary markets that function well for two reasons. Although companies actually raise new capital in the primary markets, the secondary markets provide the liquidity for securities sold in the primary markets, making them more attractive to buyers and sellers of these securities because they know they can be bought or sold whenever desired. Also, all companies, even those that do not raise capital through using the primary markets, can use the secondary markets to invest excess corporate funds.

Direct Your Learning

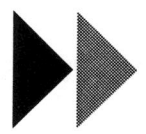

Assignment 2

Financial Statements

Educational Objectives

After learning the content of this assignment, you should be able to:

1. Explain the purpose of financial statements.
2. Explain the importance of the following:
   - General accounting concepts
   - Concepts and principles affecting the recording of transactions
   - Concepts and principles affecting the preparation of financial statements
3. Describe the content and purpose of the following primary financial statements:
   - Balance sheet
   - Income statement
   - Statement of changes in owners' equity
   - Statement of cash flows
4. Describe the relationships between the primary financial statements.
5. Describe the limitations of financial statements.
6. Explain how insurance professionals use financial statements.

Study Materials

Required Reading:
- Finance for Risk Management and Insurance Professionals
  - Chapter 2

Study Aids:
- SMART Online Practice Exams
- SMART Study Aids
  - Review Notes and Flash Cards—Assignment 2

Outline

- **Purpose of Financial Statements**
- **Accounting Concepts and Principles**
  - A. General Accounting Concepts
  - B. Concepts and Principles Affecting the Recording of Transactions
  - C. Concepts and Principles Affecting the Preparation of Financial Statements
- **Primary Financial Statements**
  - A. Balance Sheet
  - B. Income Statement
  - C. Statement of Changes in Owners' Equity
  - D. Statement of Cash Flows
- **Relationships Between Financial Statements**
- **Limitations of Financial Statements**
- **Uses of Financial Statements by Insurance Professionals**
- **Summary**

s.m.a.r.t. tips — Reduce the number of Key Words and Phrases that you must review. SMART Flash Cards contain the Key Words and Phrases and their definitions, allowing you to set aside those cards that you have mastered.

Key Words and Phrases

Define or describe each of the words and phrases listed below.

Financial statement (p. 2.3)

Accounting (p. 2.3)

Generally accepted accounting principles (GAAP) (p. 2.4)

Business entity concept (p. 2.5)

Going concern concept (p. 2.5)

Money measurement concept (p. 2.6)

Cost principle (p. 2.6)

Revenue recognition principle (p. 2.6)

Matching principle (p. 2.6)

Accrual basis accounting (p. 2.6)

Cash basis accounting (p. 2.6)

Materiality principle (p. 2.7)

Substance over form concept (p. 2.7)

Accounting period concept (p. 2.8)

Consistency principle (p. 2.8)

Conservatism principle (p. 2.8)

Balance sheet (p. 2.9)

Accounting equation (p. 2.9)

Assets (p. 2.9)

Liabilities (p. 2.10)

Owners' equity (p. 2.10)

Income statement (p. 2.11)

Revenue (p. 2.11)

Expenses (p. 2.11)

Statement of changes in owners' equity (p. 2.12)

Paid-in capital (p. 2.12)

Par value (p. 2.12)

Retained earnings (p. 2.12)

Dividends (p. 2.12)

Statement of cash flows (p. 2.12)

Review Questions

1. Identify activities that are presented quantitatively on an organization's financial statement. (p. 2.3)

2. Describe how financial information typically flows within an organization from the occurrence of financial activity to the reporting on financial statements. (pp. 2.3–2.4)

3. Identify the purpose of financial statements. (p. 2.4)

4. List individuals who might use information contained in financial statements to make informed financial decisions regarding an organization. (p. 2.4)

5. Describe the following guidelines used in interpreting and assessing an organization's financial condition and performance:
   a. Accounting concepts (p. 2.4)

   b. Accounting principles (p. 2.4)

6. Identify the categories of concepts and principles encompassed by generally accepted accounting principles (GAAP). (p. 2.5)

7. Describe the assumptions made when analyzing financial statements according to the following key accounting concepts:
   a. Business entity concept (p. 2.5)

   b. Going concern concept (p. 2.5)

8. Describe the following concepts and principles that help a user of financial statements understand information contained in transaction records:
   - Money measurement concept (p. 2.6)

   - Cost principle (p. 2.6)

   - Revenue recognition principle (p. 2.6)

   - Matching principle (p. 2.6)

   - Materiality principle (p. 2.7)

   - Substance over form concept (p. 2.7)

9. Compare accrual basis accounting and cash basis accounting regarding the recognition of revenue on financial statements. (p. 2.6)

10. Describe the following concepts and principles that help an organization prepare a conservative and consistent presentation of financial information:
    - Accounting period concept (p. 2.8)

    - Consistency principle (p. 2.8)

    - Conservatism principle (p. 2.8)

11. Describe the following four primary financial statements.
    (1) Balance sheet (pp. 2.9–2.10)

(2) Income statement (p. 2.11)

(3) Statement of changes in owners' equity (p. 2.12)

(4) Statement of cash flows (pp. 2.12–2.13)

12. Describe the elements within an organization's capital accounts as reflected in the statement of changes in owners' equity. (p. 2.12)

13. Describe the three sections of organizational activities summarized in the statement of cash flows. (p. 2.13)

14. Explain why it is important to analyze an entire set of financial statements together to develop an overall evaluation of an organization's financial status. (pp. 2.14–2.15)

15. Explain why the accuracy of financial statements is limited. (p. 2.16)

16. Identify the significant limitations in the accuracy of financial statements. (p. 2.16)

17. Explain how an organization's quantitative and qualitative assets are presented in financial statements. (p. 2.16)

18. Explain how the cost principle of accounting limits the accuracy of the financial reporting of an organization's current fair market value of assets. (pp. 2.16–2.17)

19. Identify how the following insurance professionals might use the information contained in financial statements:

   a. Company management (p. 2.17)

   b. Agent or broker (p. 2.17)

   c. Underwriter (p. 2.17)

   d. Claim representative (p. 2.18)

Application Questions

1. Assume two companies have completed the same financial transactions, as indicated below. The only difference is that Company A uses the cash basis of accounting and Company B uses the accrual basis of accounting. Determine the net income each company will show on its income statement for the month ended 6/30/XX.

Transaction	Date	Amount
Purchased 100 widgets	5/15/XX	$10,000
Sold 50 widgets for cash	6/10/XX	7,500
Sold 50 widgets on credit	6/19/XX	7,500
Received cash on credit sale	7/19/XX	7,500

	Company A	Company B
Sales	7,500	15,000
Cost of Goods Sold		10,000
Net Income	7,500	5,000

2. Listed below are financial statement accounts. Indicate in the spaces to the right of each account its category and the financial statement or statements in which it can usually be found. Use the following abbreviations:

Category		Financial Statement	
Asset	A	Balance Sheet	BS
Liability	L	Income Statement	IS
Owners' Equity	OE	Statement of Changes in Owners' Equity	SOE
Revenue	R	Statement of Cash Flows	SCF
Expense	E		
Gain	G		
Loss	LS		

	Category	Financial Statement
Cash	Asset	BS
Accounts payable	Liability	BS
Common stock	Owners' Equity	BS
Depreciation expense	Expense	IS SCF
Net sales	Revenue	IS
Income tax expense	Expense	IS
Short-term investments	Asset	BS
Equipment purchase	Asset	BS SCF
Retained earnings	Owners' Equity	SOE
Accounts receivable	Asset	BS
Short-term debt	Liability	BS

3. The information below presents selected data from three different companies' balance sheets and income statements for the year ended December 31, 20XX. Calculate the missing amounts.

	Company A	Company B	Company C
Total assets, 12/31/XX	$290,000	$460,000	$630,000
Total liabilities, 12/31/XX	$80,000	184,000	270,000
Paid-in capital, 12/31/XX	55,000	90,000	140,000
Retained earnings, 12/31/XX	155,000?	186,000	220,000
Net income, for 20XX	105,000	84,000	72,000
Dividends declared and paid in 20XX	20,000	50,000	28,000
Retained earnings, 1/1/XX	70,000	152,000	176,000?

TOTAL ASSETS = TOTAL LIABILITIES + PAID-IN CAPITAL + ENDING RETAINED EARNINGS

ENDING RETAINED EARNINGS = BEGINNING RETAINED EARNINGS + NET INCOME − DIVIDENDS

4. The balance sheet of KAO Enterprises includes a building with a value of $1 million. Should an underwriter use this figure as the value of the building for determining insurance coverage needs? Why or why not?

5. Assume that you are an underwriter for the XYZ Insurance Company and that the marketing department has asked you to appoint the ABC Insurance Agency to represent your company.

Why might you ask for the agency's financial statements, and what information would you be looking for?

Answers to Assignment 2 Questions

NOTE: These answers are provided to give students a basic understanding of acceptable types of responses. They often are not the only valid answers and are not intended to provide an exhaustive response to the questions.

Review Questions

1. Activities that are quantitatively presented on an organization's financial statement include sales, purchases, borrowings, repayments, and investments.

2. Financial information typically flows as follows within an organization:
   (1) Financial activity occurs.
   (2) Information regarding the activity is forwarded to the accounting department:
   - Record activity using bookkeeping.
   - Classify, analyze, and determine appropriate method of reporting the effects of the bookkeeping records in the financial statements.
   - Prepare financial statements using standardized accounting concepts and principles.

3. The purpose of financial statements is to communicate information about an organization's financial activities, and the results of those activities, to individuals who need to make informed financial decisions about the organization.

4. Individuals who might use information contained in financial statements to make informed financial decisions regarding an organization include management, investors, insurers, and employees.

5. The following guidelines are used in interpreting and assessing an organization's financial condition and performance:
   a. Accounting concepts—Represent the underlying assumptions and rules of measurement of accounting theory
   b. Accounting principles—Standards or methods for presenting financial information that have been developed through accounting practice or established by industry organizations

6. Generally accepted accounting principles (GAAP) encompass the following categories of concepts and principles:
   - General accounting concepts
   - Concepts and principles affecting the recording of transactions
   - Concepts and principles affecting the preparation of financial statements

7. The following assumptions are made when analyzing financial statements according to general accounting concepts:
   a. Business entity concept—Assumes that each organization, or business entity, has an existence separate from its owners, creditors, employees, and other businesses. Financial statements report only resources, obligations, and results of the activities of the business entity.
   b. Going concern concept—Assumes that a business entity will continue to operate indefinitely. This assumption affects the values assigned to assets recorded in an organization's financial statements.

8. The following concepts and principles help a user understand information contained in transaction records:
    - Money measurement concept—Identifies that organizations must report economic activities in money terms.
    - Cost principle—Identifies that all organizations record their assets at historical cost.
    - Revenue recognition principle—Identifies how organizations recognize their revenue.
    - Matching principle—Identifies that organizations record expenses incurred in generating revenues in the same time period in which those revenues are recorded.
    - Materiality principle—Identifies that accountants can ignore GAAP when recording items that are not material if to do so is less expensive and more convenient.
    - Substance over form concept—Identifies that transactions are recorded in a way that reflects their economic substance and not simply their legal form.
9. Under accrual basis accounting, revenues and expenses are recorded as they are incurred rather than when cash is received or paid. This requires the use of account receivable and account payable accounts. Cash basis accounting records transactions only as cash is received or paid.
10. The following concepts and principles help an organization prepare a conservative and consistent presentation of financial information:
    - Accounting period concept—Requires financial statements to be prepared over relatively short time periods so users can make valid comparisons of information from period to period.
    - Consistency principle—Requires an organization to use the same accounting principles and reporting practices in every accounting period. Alternatively, it may change methods and practices, as long as the change is disclosed, along with the reasons for the change and its effect on current and cumulative prior years' income.
    - Conservatism principle—Requires transactions to be recorded in a manner such that net assets and net income are not overstated to ensure that the costs of generating specific revenues are recorded in the same accounting period as the revenues are recorded.
11. The following four financial statements present an organization's overall financial status and results of operations:
    (1) Balance sheet—Provides a snapshot of a company's financial position as of a specific date, and records the assets, liabilities, and owners' equity as of that date.
    (2) Income statement—Reports an organization's profit or loss for a stated period and helps identify types of operations the organization is performing and whether they are profitable enough to keep the organization in business.
    (3) Statement of changes in owners' equity—Explains any changes that have occurred in the organization's capital accounts during a specific period, and indicates how much of the net income is being reinvested for ongoing future business needs.
    (4) Statement of cash flows—Summarizes the cash effects of an organization's operating, investing, and financing activities during a specified period. Used to determine an organization's ability to generate positive future cash flows, ability to meet financial obligations, need for additional financing, and reasons for any differences between net income and associated cash receipts and disbursements.

12. The elements that constitute an organization's capital accounts include:
    - The total amount invested in the organization by the owners, as represented by paid-in capital.
    - The cumulative net income that an organization has retained after paying dividends and reinvesting in the organization's operations, as represented by retained earnings.
13. The following three sections of activities are summarized in the statement of cash flows:
    (1) Operating activities—Reflects operating cash inflows and operating cash outflows. Non-cash income and non-cash expenses are not included.
    (2) Investing activities—Reflects actual cash inflows and outflows that have occurred as a result of activities such as sale or purchase of property, plant, or equipment; acquisition or disposal of marketable securities; and receipt of payments on loans made to others.
    (3) Financing activities—Reports cash inflows and outflows that have occurred as a result of activities such as issuing or repurchasing stock, bonds, or mortgages.
14. It is important to analyze an entire set of financial statements together because, taken together, the financial statements provide the user with a snapshot of the financial condition of the organization at the end of the fiscal year, along with a summary of the financial effects of business activities during the current reporting period.
15. The accuracy of financial statements is limited because many estimates, assumptions, and compromises are required in the process of preparing the documents.
16. The following are significant limitations in the accuracy of financial statements:
    - They do not measure the economic value of an organization's qualitative assets.
    - They do not give the current fair market value of the organization's assets for determining its true worth.
17. Quantitative economic data are presented in the financial statements. Qualitative assets typically have no measurement value assigned and are not presented in financial statements; however, an exception is the value given to assets that have been purchased as part of an acquisition of another organization. These qualitative assets are recorded as goodwill in the financial statements of the purchasing company.
18. The accuracy of financial reporting of current fair market value of an organization's assets is limited (1) because the cost principle of accounting requires assets to be recorded at the price agreed on at the time of exchange, which does not consider inflation, and (2) because of depreciation charges, which reflect historical costs, not replacement costs.
19. Insurance professionals might use information contained in financial statements for the following purposes:
    a. Company management—To help make informed decisions regarding their areas of responsibility and to monitor the results of the decisions with an eye toward fulfilling the goal of maximizing shareholder value.
    b. Agent or broker—To identify potential loss exposures or financial liabilities that are neither insured nor adequately addressed by risk management techniques and to identify trends in an organization's performance that signal potential problems or growth opportunities.
    c. Underwriter—To assess an applicant's financial stability in the context of acceptability for coverage.

d. Claim representative—To identify the possibility of a moral hazard related to a claim and to calculate the amount of a claim settlement.

Application Questions

1. | Income Statement | Company A | Company B |
    |---|---|---|
    | Sales | $7,500 | $15,000 |
    | Cost of goods sold | 0 | 10,000 |
    | Net income | $ 7,500 | $5,000 |

    Because Company A is on the cash basis, it recorded the purchase of the 100 widgets as an expense in May when they were paid for and recorded the credit sale of 50 widgets in July when the cash was received.

    Company B, using the accrual basis, has a better matching of revenue and expenses. The 100 widgets purchased were carried in inventory until they were sold. The revenue from sales was recorded when the sale took place. The credit sale was carried in accounts receivable until the cash was collected.

2. | | | |
    |---|---|---|
    | Cash | A | BS |
    | Accounts payable | L | BS |
    | Common stock | OE | BS |
    | Depreciation expense | E | IS SCF |
    | Net sales | R | IS |
    | Income tax expense | E | IS |
    | Short-term investments | A | BS |
    | Equipment purchase | A | BS SCF |
    | Retained earnings | OE | SOE |
    | Accounts receivable | A | BS |
    | Short-term debt | L | BS |

3. | | Company A | Company B | Company C |
    |---|---|---|---|
    | Total assets, 12/31/XX | $290,000 | $460,000 | $630,000 |
    | Total liabilities, 12/31/XX | 80,000 | 184,000 | 270,000 |
    | Paid-in capital, 12/31/XX | 55,000 | 90,000 | 140,000 |
    | Retained earnings, 12/31/XX | 155,000 | 186,000 | 220,000 |
    | Net income, for 20XX | 105,000 | 84,000 | 72,000 |
    | Dividends declared and paid in 20XX | 20,000 | 50,000 | 28,000 |
    | Retained earnings, 1/1/XX | 70,000 | 152,000 | 176,000 |

Step-by-step calculations using the following formulas:

Total assets = Total liabilities + Paid-in capital + Ending retained earnings.

Ending retained earnings = Beginning retained earnings + Net income − Dividends.

Company A

Total assets = $80,000 + $55,000 + ($70,000 + $105,000 − $20,000)

= $135,000 + $155,000

= $290,000.

Company B

$460,000 = Total liabilities + $90,000 + $186,000

$460,000 = Total liabilities + $276,000

Total liabilities = $460,000 − $276,000

= $184,000.

$186,000 = $152,000 + $84,000 − Dividends

$186,000 = $236,000 − Dividends

Dividends = $236,000 − $186,000

= $50,000.

Company C

$630,000 = $270,000 + $140,000 + Ending retained earnings

$630,000 = $410,000 + Ending retained earnings

Ending retained earnings = $630,000 − $410,000

Ending retained earnings = $220,000.

$220,000 = Beginning retained earnings + $72,000 − $28,000

$220,000 = Beginning retained earnings + $44,000

Beginning retained earnings = $220,000 − $44,000

= $176,000.

4. No, the underwriter should not use the value of the building as stated on the balance sheet for determining the amount of insurance coverage needed. The value of the building on the balance sheet is the amount KAO Enterprises paid for the building. It is likely that the value of the building has changed since it was purchased. Therefore, an appraisal or some other valuation method should be applied to determine the insurable value.

5. Insurers want to appoint agents who are business professionals capable of earning a profit and who will stay in business selling insurance for many years. A balance sheet will show the relationship between an agent's assets, liabilities, and owners' equity. Comparing balance sheets at the end of the year for several years will show changes in assets and liabilities as well as the components of an agent's assets and liabilities. Any large differences should be explained.

The income statement is also useful in determining whether the agent's flow of commission income is sufficient to meet all operating expenses with some left over to add to owners' equity. Because agents are usually authorized to bind coverage and collect premiums on behalf of the insurance company, insurers want to know whether an agency manages its finances effectively. A profitable agency that adds to owners' equity each year is likely to stay in business, abide by contractual agreements to remit premiums to insurers in a timely manner, and treat customers fairly. Agents with declining owners' equity might find it difficult to stay in business for many years.

Direct Your Learning

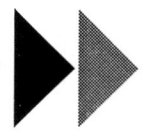

ASSIGNMENT 3

Sources of Additional Financial and Nonfinancial Information

Educational Objectives

After learning the content of this assignment, you should be able to:

1. Explain how the following levels of the outside accountants' service affect the reliability of financial statements:
   - No involvement
   - Compilation
   - Review
   - Audit

2. Explain why notes to financial statements are considered an integral part of a company's financial statements and how they explain or amplify the information contained in the statements.

3. Explain why the content of a company's annual report is important to financial statement users and how the content meets the information needs of its users.

4. Explain how to access and use company information filed with the Securities and Exchange Commission.

5. Describe the following additional sources of financial information and the information that they provide to financial analysts:
   - Rating agencies
   - Credit bureaus
   - Analyst reports
   - News articles

Study Materials

Required Reading:
- Finance for Risk Management and Insurance Professionals
  - Chapter 3

Study Aids:
- SMART Online Practice Exams
- SMART Study Aids
  - Review Notes and Flash Cards—Assignment 3

Outline

▶ **Outside Accountants' Level of Service**
   A. No Involvement
   B. Compilation
   C. Review
   D. Audit

▶ **Notes to the Financial Statements**
   A. Nature of Operations
   B. Significant Accounting Policies
   C. Long-Term Debt and Other Commitments
   D. Contingencies
   E. Financial Information by Business Segment
   F. Other Explanations

▶ **Company Annual Reports**
   A. Required Information
      1. Report of Management
      2. Management's Discussion and Analysis of Results
      3. Selected Financial Data
   B. Additional Information
      1. Financial Highlights
      2. Letter to Shareholders
      3. Corporate Message

▶ **Securities and Exchange Commission Filings**
   A. Form 10-K
   B. Form 10-Q
   C. Form 8-K
   D. Electronic Data Gathering, Analysis, and Retrieval System (EDGAR)

▶ **Additional Sources of Financial Information**
   A. Rating Agencies
   B. Credit Bureaus
   C. Analyst Reports
   D. News Articles

▶ **Summary**

s.m.a.r.t. tips

Actively capture information by using the open space in the SMART Review Notes to write out key concepts. Putting information into your own words is an effective way to push that information into your memory.

Key Words and Phrases
Define or describe each of the words and phrases listed below.

Accountant's report (p. 3.4)

Compilation (p. 3.5)

Review (p. 3.6)

Audit (p. 3.6)

Notes to the financial statements (p. 3.9)

Transparency (p. 3.15)

Selected financial data (p. 3.16)

Review Questions

1. Describe information typically provided by the accountant's report. (p. 3.4)

2. Describe the required contents of a publicly traded company's annual auditing report, as mandated by the Sarbanes-Oxley Act of 2002. (p. 3.7)

3. Explain the indications of the following accountant opinions regarding the accuracy of a company's financial statements:
   a. Unqualified opinion (p. 3.7)

   b. Qualified opinion (p. 3.7)

   c. Adverse opinion (p. 3.9)

d. Disclaimer of opinion (p. 3.9)

4. Describe information contained in the following notes to financial statements:

   a. Nature of operations (p. 3.10)

   b. Significant accounting policies (pp. 3.10–3.12)

   c. Long-term debt and other commitments (p. 3.12)

   d. Contingencies (p. 3.12)

   e. Financial information by business segment (p. 3.13)

f. Other explanations (p. 3.13)

5. Describe why the following accounting methods and procedures might be significant to financial statement users:
   a. Consolidation of results of subsidiaries (p. 3.10)

   b. Valuation of inventories (pp. 3.10–3.11)

   c. Recognition of revenue (p. 3.11)

   d. Depreciation of long-term assets (p. 3.11)

   e. Recording of income taxes (p. 3.11)

f. Treatment of employee benefit plans (p. 3.11)

g. Calculation of earnings per share (p. 3.12)

6. Identify factors that a company might use to group business and create business segments. (p. 3.13)

7. Explain the usefulness of a company annual report to an insurance professional. (p. 3.13)

8. Describe the annual report sections required by the U.S. Securities and Exchange Commission (SEC). (pp. 3.14–3.16)

9. Identify the three areas of disclosure regarding the SEC's interpretive guidelines for MD&A prompted by Sarbanes-Oxley. (p. 3.15)

10. Describe the information contained in the additional information section of a company's annual report. (pp. 3.16, 3.18)

11. Identify the SEC financial filings required of all publicly traded companies. (p. 3.18)

12. Describe the filing forms commonly accessed by the users of financial statements through the SEC's Electronic Data Gathering, Analysis, and Retrieval (EDGAR) system. (pp. 3.18–3.19)

13. List the events that trigger an 8-K filing with the SEC. (p. 3.19)

14. Explain why the information provided by rating agencies is important to a company. (pp. 3.20–3.21)

15. Describe two types of ratings issued by rating agencies and the typical users of these ratings. (p. 3.21)

16. Identify the quantitative and qualitative financial factors rating agencies use to develop their ratings. (p. 3.21)

Application Questions

1. Included in the information an underwriter receives from a company applying for insurance coverage is a set of the company's financial statements. There is no report from an outside accountant attached to the financial statements. How should the underwriter consider the information contained in these financial statements?

2. As part of a policy renewal review, a thorough analysis of the quantitative data in an insured company's current financial statements indicates that the company is well capitalized and extremely profitable. Why is it important to also review the notes to the financial statements before making final assessment of the insured's financial condition?

3. An insurer's investment portfolio manager is considering making an investment in the common stock of a publicly traded company. What additional information is included in the company's annual report, and how can it be useful to the portfolio manager when making the investment decision?

4. The portfolio manager must make his investment decision on March 15, 20X1. The information in the annual report is as of December 31, 20X0. How can the portfolio manager determine whether any major events affecting the company have occurred since the date of the annual report?

5. In addition to doing his own research into the company, the portfolio manager would also like to consider analyst reports from several broker-dealers. However, he is concerned about the potential for conflict-of-interest issues when analysts make buy or sell recommendations. How does the Sarbanes-Oxley Act of 2002 address these concerns?

Answers to Assignment 3 Questions

NOTE: These answers are provided to give students a basic understanding of acceptable types of responses. They often are not the only valid answers and are not intended to provide an exhaustive response to the questions.

Review Questions

1. The accountant's report explains the accountant's level of service provided in the preparation of a company's financial statements and any opinion statement regarding those financial statements. The accountant's report provides the financial statement user with a basis for making a decision about how much reliance to place on the financial statement.

2. The Sarbanes-Oxley Act of 2002 mandates publicly traded companies to include the following in the annual auditing report:
   - Management's responsibility for establishing and maintaining internal controls over its financial reporting
   - Management's evaluation of the effectiveness of such internal controls
   - An opinion from outside accountants on management's evaluation of its internal controls
   - An evaluation of the accounting principles used
   - An evaluation of significant estimates made by management
   - An evaluation of overall financial statement presentation

3. Accountant opinions regarding the accuracy of the financial statements include the following:
   a. Unqualified opinion—The financial statements as a whole present a fair representation of the company's financial position and results of operations for the period audited.
   b. Qualified opinion—Makes a limited exception to the conclusion that the financial statements are a fair representation of the company's financial position and results of operations for the period audited.
   c. Adverse opinion—Sufficient evidence was obtained to perform the required audit, and that evidence shows that the financial statements do not fairly present the company's financial position and results of operations.
   d. Disclaimer of opinion—Accountant has not been able to obtain sufficient evidence to express an opinion. The disclaimer must include the reasons for which no opinion was given.

4. The following information is included in notes to the financial statements:
   a. Nature of operations—Contains information about the company's industry, type of business, products and services offered, scope of the operations, and size, and any individual entities that are part of the company.
   b. Significant accounting policies—Identifies the accounting policies and procedures the company has adopted. Financial statement users can make more informed comparisons of the financial position and results of different companies within the same industry.
   c. Long-term debt and other commitments—Identifies the type, maturity, and interest rates of the long-term debt securities issued by the company. Allows financial statement users to assess the company's future cash needs and its ability to meet them, and to determine the probable effect on income of interest rate changes.

d. Contingencies—Discloses possible exposures to loss and liability.
e. Financial information by business segment—Highlights the company's risks and returns and shows the financial position and performance of each business segment.
f. Other explanations—Provides additional information to ensure full disclosure and provide information that users of financial statements need to make informed business decisions.

5. The following accounting methods and procedures are significant to disclose to the financial statement users:
   a. Consolidation of results of subsidiaries—Significant assets and liabilities could be omitted from financial statements, possibly affecting risk management programs.
   b. Valuation of inventories—Method used affects the decision regarding amounts of insurance coverage estimated to cover inventories and the cost of goods sold expense, ultimately affecting the net income figure.
   c. Recognition of revenue—Method used can be an important consideration in adjusting a claim that arises under business income coverage.
   d. Depreciation of long-term assets—Depreciation affects the balance sheet, the income statement, and, ultimately, the net income.
   e. Recording of income taxes—Income taxes affect the company's net income, and it is important to understand how aggressively the company interprets the tax code when calculating its income taxes.
   f. Treatment of employee benefit plans—Unfunded pension costs can represent a significant future liability of the company.
   g. Calculation of earnings per share—Because earnings per share is used by the investment community to value stock, it is important to understand how EPS is calculated.

6. A company might create business segments by using the following factors:
   - Nature of the products and services
   - Production processes
   - Types of customers for the products and services
   - Methods of distributing the products or providing the services
   - Regulatory environment
   - Geographical considerations, such as:
     - Economic and political conditions
     - Proximity of operations
     - Special risks associated with operations in a particular area
     - Underlying currency risks
     - Regulations

7. A company annual report is useful to an insurance professional because it provides information about the company's business purpose and philosophy, its financial results, and its direction for the future. This information provides background for making underwriting decisions.

8. The following sections of the annual report are required by the U.S. Securities and Exchange Commission (SEC):
   - Financial statements and notes—Current figures along with descriptions of the accounting methods, procedures, and estimates that a particular company uses
   - Auditor's report—Report that expresses an accountant's professional opinion about whether the financial statements fairly represent the financial condition of the company
   - Report of management—Acknowledges management's responsibility for the quality and integrity of the company's financial statements and the adequacy and effectiveness of the internal controls over financial reporting; is signed by the chairman of the board and chief financial officer
   - Management's discussion and analysis of results of operations and financial condition—Focuses on explaining the company's operating results and condition, and provides insight into the material opportunities, challenges, and risks the company faces.
   - Selected financial data—Highlights certain significant trends in the company's financial condition and results of operations.

9. Sarbanes-Oxley prompted the following three areas of disclosure regarding the SEC's interpretive guidance for MD&A:
   (1) Liquidity and capital resources
   (2) Certain trading activities involving non-exchange traded contracts accounted for at fair market value
   (3) Relationships and transactions with persons or entities that derive benefits from non-independent relationships with the company or the company's related parties

10. Information that might be presented in the additional information section of a company's annual report includes the following:
    - Financial highlights—Contains a brief summary of the company's results for the year
    - Letter to shareholders—Provides a review and analysis of the significant events of the year and typically addresses any issues and successes the company experienced
    - Corporate message—Explains the company's mission, lines of business, corporate culture, and strategic direction

11. SEC financial filings required of all publicly traded companies include quarterly and annual financial information and notice of any potential material events that might affect the company's financial condition.

12. The users of financial statements frequently access the following filing forms through the SEC's EDGAR system:
    - Form 10-K—An annual report, similar to a company's own annual report, containing more-detailed information about the company's business, finances, and management
    - Form 10-Q—A quarterly report filed for each of the first three quarters of the fiscal year containing unaudited financial statements, an MD&A for the quarter, and a list of material events that have occurred within the company during the prior three months
    - Form 8-K—A current report filed within four days of a triggering event that announces major events that shareholders should know about

13. The following events trigger an 8-K filing with the SEC:
    - Material definitive agreements entered into or terminated that are not in the ordinary course of the company's business
    - Release of nonpublic information about a company's financial condition
    - Creation of a direct financial obligation under an off balance sheet arrangement
    - Change of independent auditor certifying the financial statements
    - Departure or election of directors and departure or appointment of principal officers

14. The ratings provided by rating agencies are important to a company because they affect the perceived risk incorporated into interest rates that apply to bonds issued by and loans made to companies.

15. Rating agencies typically issue the following two types of ratings:
    (1) Claims-paying and/or financial strength ratings—Assess an insurer's ability to meet its financial obligations to policyholders
    (2) Credit ratings—Assess a company's prospects for repaying its debts

    Customers usually focus on claims-paying ratings, creditors focus on debt ratings, and investors use both ratings.

16. Quantitative financial factors used by rating agencies to develop their ratings include profit margins, financial leverage, liquidity, cash flows, and capital and surplus ratios.

    Qualitative financial factors used by rating agencies to develop their ratings include underwriting cycle, competitive environment, regulatory and political factors, soundness of reinsurance, adequacy of reserves, quality of invested assets, and management experience and accomplishments.

Application Questions

1. If no accountant's report is attached to a set of financial statements, the underwriter should assume the financial statements have been completed by the company with no involvement from its outside accountant. As users of these financial statements, underwriters must—based on their knowledge of the company, its management, and the industry—make their own judgments as to the quality and integrity of the information provided.

2. In addition to reviewing the financial information included in a set of financial statements, it is important to review the notes to the financial statements. These notes include information that is better provided, or that can only be provided, in the form of notes to explain or amplify the information presented in the financial statements. The information provided in the notes is essential to understanding the financial statements; therefore, these notes are considered an integral part of financial statements prepared in accordance with generally accepted accounting principles.

3. In addition to reading the financial data in a company's annual report, the portfolio manager should review the Report of Management, Management's Discussion and Analysis of Results, and the corporate message. The Report of Management is a report to the users of the financial statements, signed by the chairman of the board and the chief financial officer, in which the company's management acknowledges its responsibility for the quality and integrity of the company's financial statements and for the adequacy of internal controls over financial reporting. Management's Discussion and Analysis of Results provides a narrative explanation of the company's financial statements that enables users to view the company from management's perspective. It improves

overall financial disclosure and provides the context within which financial statements can be analyzed. It also provides information about the quality and variability of the company's income and cash flow, so that users can ascertain the likelihood that past performance indicates future performance. The company uses its corporate message section to explain the company's mission, lines of business, corporate culture, and strategic direction. This section is often considered an advertisement for the company; however, it does provide insight into how the company perceives itself in the marketplace and how it would like the users of the annual report to perceive it.

4. To determine whether any major events have occurred that affected the company since the publication of its annual report, the portfolio manager should obtain a copy of any Form 8-K that the company has filed with the Securities and Exchange Commission since the end of 20X0. Form 8-K is the current report that publicly traded companies must file with the SEC to announce any major events that shareholders should know about. This form must be filed within four business days of the triggering event. Form 8-K can be accessed through the SEC's Web site using its electronic data gathering, analysis, and retrieval system (EDGAR).

5. As part of the Sarbanes-Oxley Act of 2002, in an attempt to address analyst conflict-of-interest issues, the SEC now requires all analyst reports issued by broker-dealers to include the following two statements:

   (1) The research analyst, or analysts, must certify that the views expressed in the analyst's report accurately reflect the research analyst's opinion about the security and issuer.

   (2) The research analyst, or analysts, must certify either (1) that no part of his or her compensation was, is, or will be directly or indirectly related to the specific recommendation or views contained in the research report; or (2) that part or all of the analyst's compensation will be directly or indirectly related to the specific recommendations or views contained in the paper. If the compensation is related to the recommendation or views, the statement must include the source, amount, and purpose of such compensation and further disclose that it may influence the report's recommendations.

Direct Your Learning

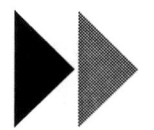

Assignment 4

Financial Statement Analysis

Educational Objectives

After learning the content of this assignment, you should be able to:

1. Explain how each of the following steps in the financial statement analysis process is accomplished:
   - Establish goals
   - Review financial statements and other information
   - Select appropriate techniques
   - Apply appropriate techniques
   - Interpret results

2. Explain how the two types of vertical analysis are used when analyzing financial statements.

3. Explain how horizontal analysis is used to evaluate a company's financial changes over time.

4. Given appropriate data, calculate and interpret financial ratios used to evaluate the following:
   - Profitability
   - Efficiency
   - Liquidity
   - Leverage

5. Describe the limitations of ratio analysis.

Study Materials

Required Reading:
- Finance for Risk Management and Insurance Professionals
  - Chapter 4

Study Aids:
- SMART Online Practice Exams
- SMART Study Aids
  - Review Notes and Flash Cards—Assignment 4

Outline

- **Analysis Process**
    - A. Establish the Goals of the Analysis
        1. Screening
        2. Evaluation
        3. Diagnosis
        4. Forecasting
        5. Reconstruction
    - B. Review the Financial Statements and Other Information
    - C. Select the Appropriate Analysis Techniques
    - D. Apply the Appropriate Analysis Techniques
    - E. Interpret the Results
- **Vertical Analysis**
    - A. Single-Period Vertical Analysis
    - B. Multiple-Period Vertical Analysis
- **Horizontal Analysis**
- **Ratio Analysis**
    - A. Evaluating Profitability
        1. Net Profit Margin
        2. Return on Assets
        3. Return on Equity
        4. DuPont Identity
        5. Combined Ratio
        6. Investment Yield Ratio
        7. Return on Policyholders' Surplus
    - B. Evaluating Efficiency
        1. Accounts Receivable Turnover Ratio
        2. Inventory Turnover Ratio
    - C. Evaluating Liquidity
        1. Working Capital
        2. Current Ratio
        3. Acid-Test Ratio
        4. Liquidity Ratio
    - D. Evaluating Leverage
        1. Debt-to-Equity Ratio
        2. Debt-to-Assets Ratio
        3. Premium-to-Surplus Ratio
        4. Reserves-to-Surplus Ratio
    - E. Limitations of Ratio Analysis
- **Summary**

Use the SMART Online Practice Exams to test your understanding of the course material. You can review questions over a single assignment or multiple assignments, or you can take an exam over the entire course. The questions are scored, and you are shown your results. (You score essay exams yourself.)

Key Words and Phrases

Define or describe each of the words and phrases listed below.

Forecasting (p. 4.6)

Common-size statement (p. 4.9)

Vertical analysis (p. 4.9)

Horizontal analysis (p. 4.9)

Gross profit margin (p. 4.15)

Net profit margin (p. 4.17)

Return on assets (ROA) (p. 4.23)

Return on equity (ROE) (p. 4.24)

DuPont identity (p. 4.24)

Asset turnover (p. 4.24)

Equity multiplier (p. 4.25)

Combined ratio (p. 4.26)

Loss ratio (p. 4.26)

Financial basis expense ratio (p. 4.26)

Trade basis expense ratio (p. 4.26)

Investment yield ratio (p. 4.27)

Return on policyholders' surplus (p. 4.28)

Accounts receivable turnover ratio (p. 4.29)

Days sales outstanding (p. 4.29)

Inventory turnover ratio (p. 4.30)

Current ratio (p. 4.31)

Acid-test ratio, or quick ratio (p. 4.32)

Liquidity ratio (p. 4.32)

Debt-to-equity ratio (p. 4.34)

Debt-to-assets ratio, or debt ratio (p. 4.35)

Premium-to-surplus ratio (p. 4.35)

Reserves-to-surplus ratio (p. 4.36)

Insurance leverage (p. 4.36)

Review Questions

1. Identify the steps in the financial statement analysis process. (pp. 4.4–4.11)

2. Describe the goals that guide a financial statement analysis. (pp. 4.4–4.6)

3. Describe the activities an analyst should perform to draw meaningful conclusions from the review of a company's financial statements. (pp. 4.6–4.8)

4. Explain how the following techniques are used to analyze financial statements:
   a. Common-size statements (p. 4.9)

b. Vertical analysis (p. 4.9)

c. Horizontal analysis (p. 4.9)

5. Describe the usefulness of the common-size statement format when performing vertical analysis. (p. 4.11)

6. Explain why it is important for the analyst to have an understanding of the company being reviewed using vertical analysis. (p. 4.14)

7. Explain how multiple-period vertical analysis might be helpful to the following insurance professionals:
   a. Underwriters (p. 4.15)

b. Loss adjusters (p. 4.15)

8. Describe the following percentage indicators used in analyzing financial statements:
   a. Gross profit margin (p. 4.15)

   b. Net profit margin (p. 4.17)

9. Identify capital structure trends an analyst might expect to see when performing vertical analysis of a company implementing a strong growth strategy. (p. 4.17)

10. Identify the focus of multiple-period vertical analysis of financial statements. (p. 4.17)

11. Describe the two methods of conducting horizontal analysis of financial statements. (p. 4.18)

12. Identify the major income statement components on which the analyst focuses when conducting horizontal analysis. (p. 4.18)

13. Describe the following GAAP-based ratios used to examine a company's profitability, and indicate how to calculate each.
    a. Net profit margin (pp. 4.22–4.23)

    b. Return on assets (p. 4.23)

    c. Return on equity (p. 4.24)

d. DuPont identity (pp. 4.24–4.26)

14. Describe the following SAP-based ratios used to examine a company's profitability:
    a. Combined ratio (pp. 4.26–4.27)

    b. Investment yield ratio (pp. 4.27–4.28)

    c. Return on policyholders' surplus (p. 4.28)

15. Describe the two ways of calculating the expense ratio. (pp. 4.26–4.27)

16. Describe two turnover ratios typically used in GAAP-based efficiency analysis of a noninsurer. (pp. 4.28–4.30)

17. Explain why evaluating an insurer's liquidity is important and how to calculate the liquidity ratio. (pp. 4.30; 4.32–4.33)

18. Describe the following measures for evaluating a company's financial leverage:
    a. Debt-to-equity ratio (p. 4.34–4.35)

    b. Debt-to-assets ratio (p. 4.35)

    c. Premium-to-surplus ratio (pp. 4.35–4.36)

d. Reserves-to-surplus ratio (pp. 4.36–4.37)

19. Describe the guidelines for determining the importance of specific financial ratios in financial statement analysis. (p. 4.37)

Application Questions

KAJ Manufacturing, Inc.

Balance Sheet		12/31/X1	12/31/X0
Current assets:			
Cash	6.2%	$ 25,000	$ 17,000 — 4.7%
Accounts receivable	10.7%	43,000	40,000 — 11.2%
Inventory	13.4%	54,000	45,000 — 12.6%
Total current assets	30.3%	$122,000	$102,000 — 28.5%
Other assets	69.7%	280,000	256,000 — 71.5%
Total assets	100.00%	$402,000	$358,000 — 100.0%
Current liabilities	14.9%	$ 60,000	$ 55,000 — 15.4%
Other liabilities	24.9%	100,000	110,000 — 30.7%
Total liabilities	39.8%	$160,000	$165,000 — 46.1%
Owners' equity	60.2%	242,000	193,000 — 53.9%
Total liabilities and owners' equity	100.00%	$402,000	$358,000 — 100.0%

Income Statement Year Ended		12/31/X1	12/31/X0	
Net sales	100.0%	$645,000	$587,000	100.0%
Cost of goods sold	70.0%	451,500	422,640	72.0%
Gross profit	30.0%	$193,500	$164,360	28.0%
Operating expenses	17.1%	110,000	100,000	17.0%
Earnings before interest and taxes (Operating income)	12.9%	$ 83,500	$ 64,360	11.0%
Interest expense	1.2%	8,000	8,800	1.5%
Earnings before taxes	11.7%	$ 75,500	$ 55,560	9.5%
Income taxes	4.1%	26,500	19,560	3.3%
Net income	7.6%	$ 49,000	$ 36,000	6.1%

1. Using the financial statements provided for KAJ Manufacturing, Inc., prepare a common-size balance sheet for 20X1 and 20X0.

2. Using the financial statements provided for KAJ Manufacturing, Inc., prepare a common-size income statement for 20X1.

3. Using the financial statements provided for KAJ Manufacturing, Inc., calculate each of the following financial ratios for 20X1. What assessments can you make about the operating performance of KAJ Manufacturing? When possible, compare your result to the benchmarks provided for miscellaneous manufacturing companies in Exhibit 4-10 of the text.

   a. Net profit margin = NET INCOME ÷ SALES
      49,000 ÷ 645,000
      7.6%

   b. Return on assets = NET INCOME ÷ TOTAL ASSETS
      49,000 ÷ 402,000
      12.2%

   c. Return on equity = NET INCOME ÷ OWNERS EQUITY
      49,000 ÷ 242,000
      20.2%

   d. Asset turnover = SALES ÷ TOTAL ASSETS
      645,000 ÷ 402,000
      1.60%

   e. Equity multiplier = TOTAL ASSETS ÷ OWNERS EQUITY
      402,000 ÷ 242,000
      1.66%

   f. DuPont identity   RETURN ON EQUITY = NET PROFIT MARGIN × ASSET TURNOVER × EQUITY MULTIPLIER
      7.6% × 1.60% × 1.66%
      = 20.2%

4. Using the common-size income statement you created in Question 2, answer the following questions:

   a. What portion of sales is available to pay for operating expenses?

   30% of NET SALES MADE IS AVAILABLE TO PAY FOR OPERATING EXPENSES

   b. What portion of sales is available for reinvestment in the company or payment to the owners?

   7.6% of NET SALES IS AVAILABLE FOR INVESTMENT IN THE COMPANY OR PAYMENT TO THE OWNERS

   c. What financial ratios describe the relationships in "a" and "b," above?

   a. Gross Profit Margin — % of sales remaining after deducting cost of goods sold
   b. Net Profit Margin — % of sales remaining after deducting all expenses

5. Using the financial statement information provided for KAJ Manufacturing to calculate the 20X0 to 20X1 percentage changes (horizontal analysis) in income statement items, answer the following questions.

   a. What is the rate of change in net sales?

   ($645,000 − $587,000) ÷ $587,000
   0.0988 or 9.9%

b. What is the rate of change in cost of goods sold?

$$(\$451,500 \text{ minus } \$422,640) \div \$422,640$$
$$.0683 \text{ or } 6.8\%$$

c. What is the rate of change in operating expenses?

$$\$(110,000 - 100,000) \div 100,000$$
$$0.1000 \text{ or } 10\%$$

d. What assessments can you make about the operating performance of KAJ Manufacturing?

Answers to Assignment 4 Questions

NOTE: These answers are provided to give students a basic understanding of acceptable types of responses. They often are not the only valid answers and are not intended to provide an exhaustive response to the questions.

Review Questions

1. The steps in the financial statement analysis process include the following:
   - Establish the goals of the analysis
   - Review the financial statements and other information
   - Select the appropriate analysis techniques
   - Apply the appropriate analysis techniques
   - Interpret the results

2. Any of the following goals guide a financial statement analysis:
   - Screening—Used to classify a company based on whether the company meets one or more pre-established criteria. Involves a pass-fail analysis focusing on specific financial data, applying pre-established criteria, and eliminating unqualified candidates.
   - Evaluation—May be directed at one or more of a company's areas of operating performance, such as profitability, liquidity, solvency, or efficiency, or toward a more general evaluation.
   - Diagnosis—Attempts to determine the reason for aberrant results in specific individual or related financial accounts. The scope of the analysis is limited to a set of accounts that are related to the results in question, rather than the entire operation of the company.
   - Forecasting—Projects a company's future operating results or financial condition based on historical and current information.
   - Reconstruction—Involves identifying and quantifying relationships between prior-period financial statement items in order to estimate missing data in all or part of a company's financial statements.

3. An analyst should perform the following activities to draw meaningful conclusions from the review of a company's financial statements:
   - Examine the auditor's report and any accompanying opinions or modifications
   - Review the accounting policies the company uses to prepare its financial statements
   - Gather background information from trade publications and other outside sources

4. The following techniques are used to analyze financial statements:
   a. Common-size statements—Amounts are reported as a percentage of a base figure. This technique is useful when the analysis requires evaluating the relative performance or financial condition of two or more companies, especially when those companies differ greatly in size.
   b. Vertical analysis—Common-size statements are used to highlight basic relationships among items within a single set of financial statements. This technique is used to identify expense items that rise more quickly or more slowly than the corresponding change in sales.
   c. Horizontal analysis—Uses period-to-period percentage changes identified in common-size statements to identify trends. This technique is effective for identifying trends and changes in trends for items such as total assets, sales, or net income.

5. The common-size statement format is useful in vertical analysis when the analyst intends to make inter-company comparisons because the format eliminates the differences in the sizes or nature of the companies. It also eliminates the effects of inflation when comparisons are made across time.

6. It is important for the analyst to have an understanding of the company being reviewed using vertical analysis because companies may have significantly different combinations of assets and liabilities depending on their individual corporate goals.

7. Multiple-period vertical analysis can be used to analyze interim period results and annual results. It may be helpful to insurance professionals in the following ways:
   a. Underwriters can assess an applicant's loss exposure to ensure the proper premium is charged.
   b. Loss adjusters can estimate the amount of inventory lost by reviewing inventory amounts recorded before and after a loss.

8. The following percentage indicators are used in analyzing financial statements:
   a. The gross profit margin is used as an indicator of a company's profitability. It represents the percentage of sales remaining after deducting the cost of goods sold.
   b. The net profit margin is used as an indicator of overall profitability. It represents the percentage of sales remaining after deducting all expenses.

9. An analyst performing vertical analysis of a company implementing a strong growth strategy might expect to see the following capital structure trends:
   - Changes such as increased long-term debt or increased common stock as a percentage of total assets
   - Increased operating expenses as a percentage of total sales
   - Increased amounts of property, plant, and equipment as a percentage of total assets

10. The focus of multiple-period vertical analysis of financial statements is on the composition of a company's assets and liabilities and whether changes in the composition of assets and liabilities over time are consistent with the company's business strategy.

11. The following are two methods of conducting horizontal analysis of financial statements:
    (1) Year-to-year analysis—Determines the percentage change in values for statement items between consecutive years in the period being considered.
    (2) Base-year-to-date analysis—Determines the percentage change in statement item values for each successive year relative to the earliest year of the period under consideration.

12. The analyst focuses on the following income statement components when conducting horizontal analysis:
    - Sales
    - Cost of goods sold
    - Gross profit
    - Operating expenses
    - Net income

13. The following GAAP-based ratios are used to examine a company's profitability:
    a. Net profit margin—The amount of each dollar of sales that remains after deducting all the expenses for the accounting period. The higher the percentage, the better the net profit margin. Calculated as follows:

    Net profit margin = Net income ÷ Sales.

    b. Return on assets (ROA)—A ratio that shows how well a company has used its resources. The higher the ROA, the more efficiently management has used those assets. Calculated as follows:

    ROA = Net income ÷ Total assets.

    c. Return on equity (ROE)—A ratio that shows the rate of return owners are earning on their investment. Calculated as follows:

    ROE = Net income ÷ Owners' equity

    d. DuPont identity—Analysis of ROA and ROE by breaking them down into their component ratios. ROA depends on asset turnover and net profit margin. Calculated as follows:

    Asset turnover × net profit margin = (Sales ÷ Total assets) × (Net income ÷ Sales)

    = Net income ÷ Total assets

    = Return on assets.

    ROE is broken down into operations, use of assets, and use of financial leverage. Calculated as follows:

    ROE = Net profit margin × Asset turnover × Equity multiplier

    = (Net income ÷ Sales) × (Sales ÷ Total assets) × (Total assets ÷ Owners' equity).

14. The following SAP-based ratios are used to examine a company's profitability:
    a. Combined ratio—Indicates whether an insurer has experienced an underwriting loss or gain. A combined ratio in excess of 100 percent indicates an underwriting loss. Calculated as follows:

    Combined ratio = Loss ratio + Expense ratio.

    b. Investment yield ratio—Indicates the total return on investments for an insurer's investment operations. Calculated as follows:

    Investment yield ratio = Net investment earnings ÷ Invested assets.

    c. Return on policyholders' surplus—Shows the rate of return an insurer is earning on its resources. Calculated as follows:

    Return on policyholders' surplus = Net income ÷ Policyholders' surplus.

15. The two ways of calculating the expense ratio are as follows:
    (1) Financial basis expense ratio—Relates underwriting expenses to earned premiums. Calculated as follows:

    Underwriting expenses ÷ Earned premiums.

    (2) Trade basis expense ratio—Relates underwriting expenses to written premiums. Used because SAP requires that costs are expensed as they are incurred. Calculated as follows:

    Underwriting expenses ÷ Written premiums.

16. The following are two turnover ratios typically used in GAAP-based efficiency analysis of a noninsurer:
    (1) Accounts receivable turnover ratio—Indicates how quickly a business collects the amounts owed by its customers. Typically, a high ratio indicates efficiency. Calculated as follows:

    $$\text{Credit sales} \div \text{Accounts receivable.}$$

    (2) Inventory turnover ratio—Indicates how quickly inventory is sold, generating either cash or accounts receivable. A low inventory turnover ratio may indicate inefficiency. Calculated as follows:

    $$\text{Cost of goods sold} \div \text{Inventory.}$$

17. Liquidity is a company's ability to convert assets to cash to satisfy its obligations. Evaluating an insurer's liquidity is important because of the regulatory emphasis on maintaining solvency. A value greater than one is considered favorable. Calculated as follows:

    $$\text{Liquidity ratio} = (\text{Cash} + \text{Invested assets}) \div (\text{Unearned premium reserve} + \text{Loss and LAE reserve}).$$

18. The following ratios are used to measure leverage:
    a. Debt-to-equity ratio—Measures the extent to which a company is financed by borrowing rather than by using its own funds. A ratio higher than 100 percent indicates that the company is mostly financed by debt. Calculated as follows:

    $$\text{Debt-to-equity ratio} = \text{Long-term debt} \div \text{Owners' equity.}$$

    b. Debt-to-assets ratio—Shows the extent to which a company's assets are financed by debt. A ratio less than one indicates that the company is financing most of its assets through the equity contributions of its shareholders. Calculated as follows:

    $$\text{Debt-to-assets ratio} = \text{Total liabilities} \div \text{Total assets.}$$

    c. Premium-to-surplus ratio—Indicates an insurer's financial strength by relating net written premiums to policyholders' surplus. It measures the extent to which a given level of policyholders' surplus can support a given level of premiums. Calculated as follows:

    $$\text{Premium-to-surplus ratio} = \text{Net written premiums} \div \text{Policyholders' surplus.}$$

    d. Reserves-to-surplus ratio—A measure of an insurer's ability to pay claims out of its reserves. Calculated as follows:

    $$\text{Reserves-to-surplus ratio} = (\text{Unearned premium reserve} + \text{Loss and LAE reserve}) \div \text{Policyholders' surplus.}$$

19. In financial statement analysis, there are no concrete guidelines for determining the importance of specific financial ratios or at what level they are too high or too low.

Application Questions

1. The common-size balance sheet is prepared by restating each item as a percentage of total assets.

   KAJ Manufacturing, Inc.
   Common Size

Balance Sheet	12/31/X1	12/31/X0
Current assets:		
Cash	6.2%	4.7%
Accounts receivable	10.7%	11.2%
Inventory	13.4%	12.6%
Total current assets	30.3%	28.5%
Other assets	69.7%	71.5%
Total assets	100.0%	100.0%
Current liabilities	14.9%	15.4%
Other liabilities	24.9%	30.7%
Total liabilities	39.8%	46.1%
Owners' equity	60.2%	53.9%
Total liabilities and owners' equity	100.0%	100.0%

2. The common-size income statement is prepared by restating each item as a percentage of sales.

   KAJ Manufacturing, Inc.
   Common Size

Income Statement Year Ended	12/31/X1	12/31/X0
Net sales	100.0%	100.0%
Cost of goods sold	70.0%	72.0%
Gross profit	30.0%	28.0%
Operating expenses	17.1%	17.0%
Earnings before interest and taxes (Operating income)	12.9%	11.0%
Interest expense	1.2%	1.5%
Earnings before taxes	11.7%	9.5%
Income taxes	4.1%	3.3%
Net income	7.6%	6.1%

3. a. Net profit margin = Net income ÷ Sales.
    = $49,000 ÷ $645,000
    = 7.6%.

    The net profit margin indicates that for every $1 of sales, KAJ Manufacturing is earning $0.076. The industry benchmark for net profit is $0.063. Therefore, KAJ is more profitable than expected for its industry.

    b. Return on assets = Net income ÷ Total assets
    = $49,000 ÷ $402,000
    = 12.2%.

    Return on assets indicates how profitably management has used the company's assets. The industry benchmark is 14.6 percent. Therefore, KAJ has not managed its assets as profitably as is expected for its industry.

    c. Return on equity = Net income ÷ Owners equity
    = $49,000 ÷ $242,000
    = 20.2%.

    Return on equity indicates how profitably management has used the equity the owners have in the company. The industry benchmark is 21 percent. Therefore, KAJ has not used the equity of the owners as profitably as is expected in its industry. However, its use of the equity in the company is closer to the industry benchmark than its return on assets.

    d. Asset turnover = Sales ÷ Total assets
    = $645,000 ÷ $402,000
    = 1.60.

    Asset turnover is another ratio that emphasizes the efficiency of the company's use of its assets. This ratio indicates the amount of sales dollars that is being generated by each dollar of assets the company owns. The industry benchmark is 1.40. Therefore, KAJ is generating more sales dollars per each dollar of assets it owns than is expected in its industry.

    e. Equity multiplier = Total assets ÷ Owners equity
    = $402,000 ÷ $242,000
    = 1.66%.

    Equity multiplier is a measure of the use of debt by the company to finance its assets. The higher this ratio, the more the company has used debt to finance its assets.

    f. The DuPont identity analyzes return on equity by breaking it into three areas: operations (net profit margin), use of assets (asset turnover), and use of financial leverage (equity multiplier).

    Return on equity = Net profit margin × Asset turnover × Equity multiplier
    20.2% = 7.6% × 1.60 × 1.66.

    We know that KAJ's return on equity is just below the industry benchmark, and its net profit margin and asset turnover are both higher than the industry benchmarks. Therefore, its equity multiplier must be below the industry benchmarks. This indicates that KAJ should consider increasing its use of leverage to finance its assets in order to increase its return on equity to at least the industry benchmark.

4. a. 30 percent of net sales made is available to pay for operating expenses.
   b. 7.6 percent of net sales is available for investment in the company or payment to the owners.
   c. The ratio in "a." is the gross profit margin. The ratio in "b." is the net profit margin.

5. a. Rate of change in net sales = ($645,000 − $587,000) ÷ $587,000

   = $58,000 ÷ $587,000

   = 0.0988, or 9.9%.

   b. Rate of change in cost of goods sold = ($451,500 − $422,640) ÷ $422,640

   = $28,860 ÷ $422,640

   = 0.0683, or 6.8%.

   c. Rate of change in operating expenses = ($110,000 − $100,000) ÷ $100,000

   = $10,000 ÷ $100,000

   = 0.1000, or 10.0%.

   d. Because sales increased by almost 10 percent, it would be a logical assumption that cost of goods sold would have increased by the same percentage. However, cost of goods sold increased by less than 7 percent. Therefore, KAJ was able to reduce the costs of the goods they sold, thereby increasing the gross profit percentage.

   Operating expenses increased by almost the same percentage as net sales. Therefore, KAJ was not able to increase its net profit margin by reducing operating expenses as a percentage of sales. This is an area KAJ management should analyze.

Direct Your Learning

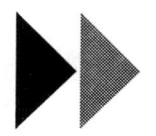

Assignment 5

Working Capital Management

Educational Objectives

After learning the content of this assignment, you should be able to:

1. Describe the typical components of working capital.
2. Explain how an insurer applies its credit policy through credit scoring and credit analysis to improve its working capital.
3. Explain how insurers make credit decisions about the following:
   - Policyholders
   - Agents and brokers
   - Reinsurers
4. Explain the following reasons that companies hold cash:
   - Transaction needs
   - Precautionary needs
   - Speculative needs
5. Describe the following cash management activities:
   - Managing float
   - Accelerating collections
   - Controlling distributions
6. Describe the following considerations for a financial manager when selecting a bank:
   - Quality
   - Service
   - Price

Study Materials

Required Reading:
- Finance for Risk Management and Insurance Professionals
  - Chapter 5

Study Aids:
- SMART Online Practice Exams
- SMART Study Aids
  - Review Notes and Flash Cards—Assignment 5

Outline

- **Working Capital**
- **Insurer Credit Management**
  - A. Credit Policy
    1. Credit Scoring
    2. Credit Analysis
  - B. Credit Decisions
    1. Policyholders
    2. Agents and Brokers
    3. Reinsurers
- **Insurer Cash Management**
  - A. Reasons for Holding Cash
  - B. Cash Management Activities
    1. Managing Float
    2. Accelerating Collections
    3. Controlling Disbursements
  - C. Considerations in Selecting a Bank
    1. Quality Considerations
    2. Service Considerations
    3. Price Considerations
- **Summary**

The SMART Online Practice Exams product contains a final practice exam. You should take this exam only when you have completed your study of the entire course. Take this exam under simulated exam conditions. It will be your best indicator of how well prepared you are.

Key Words and Phrases

Define or describe each of the words and phrases listed below.

Credit scoring (p. 5.5)

Credit analysis (p. 5.8)

Account current billing (p. 5.14)

Statement billing (p. 5.14)

Item billing (p. 5.15)

Direct billing (p. 5.15)

Float (p. 5.18)

Availability float (p. 5.19)

Processing float (p. 5.19)

Clearing float (p. 5.19)

Disbursement float (p. 5.19)

Mail float (p. 5.19)

Available balance (p. 5.19)

Net float (p. 5.19)

Lockbox (p. 5.23)

Wire transfer (p. 5.25)

Pre-authorized check (p. 5.25)

Automated Clearinghouse (ACH) (p. 5.25)

Concentration account (p. 5.26)

Zero-balance account (p. 5.26)

Draft (p. 5.28)

Compensating balance (p. 5.30)

Earnings allowance (p. 5.30)

Review Questions

1. Explain the objective of working capital management. (p. 5.3)

2. List the types of assets that are considered current for the purposes of assessing working capital. (p. 5.4)

3. Describe typical working capital decisions a financial manager makes when managing current assets. (p. 5.4)

4. Describe the purpose of a credit policy and why its implementation is important for insurers. (p. 5.5)

5. Describe how the following tools are used in applying a credit policy:
   a. Credit scoring (pp. 5.5–5.6)

   b. Credit analysis (p. 5.8)

6. Explain how a credit score is calculated using a simple credit-scoring model. (p. 5.6)

7. Describe the Z-score model and its application in credit scoring. (p. 5.7)

8. Describe how the following commonly used credit analysis tools are useful to financial managers and underwriters when evaluating an individual or organization:
   - Financial statements (p. 5.9)

   - Business credit rating services (p. 5.9)

   - Consumer credit reporting agencies (p. 5.11)

9. Identify reasons an organization might decide to extend credit. (p. 5.11)

10. List the five "C"s of credit, often used in the credit decision-making process. (p. 5.11)

11. Identify the issues for consideration when making credit decisions regarding the following entities:
    a. Policyholders (pp. 5.12–5.13)

    b. Agents and brokers (pp. 5.13–5.15)

    c. Reinsurers (pp. 5.15–5.17)

12. Describe the three primary billing plans used by producers. (pp. 5.14–5.15)

13. Explain why regulators are concerned with reporting requirements regarding reinsurance recoverables. (p. 5.16)

14. Identify short-term marketable securities that are considered cash equivalents for cash management purposes. (p. 5.17)

15. Describe the activities involved in cash management. (p. 5.17)

16. Describe reasons for which companies hold some of their assets in the form of cash. (pp. 5.17–5.18)

17. Contrast the cash operating cycles of noninsurers and insurers. (p. 5.18)

18. Explain how the following activities help track and control the flow of funds through a company:
    a. Managing float (p. 5.18)

b. Accelerating collections (pp. 5.23–5.25)

   c. Controlling disbursements (pp. 5.26–5.28)

19. Identify the components of availability and disbursement float. (p. 5.19)

20. Describe methods used to accelerate fund collections. (pp. 5.23–5.25)

21. Explain how the following accounts provide a way of avoiding the possibility of overdrafts:
    - Concentration account (p. 5.26)

    - Zero-balance account (pp. 5.26–5.27)

22. List the criteria a financial manager is likely to use in selecting a bank. (p. 5.28)

23. Identify the most important criteria a financial manager considers when selecting a bank for cash management service. (p. 5.29)

24. List possible payment methods for bank service activities. (p. 5.30)

Application Questions

1. An underwriter has been informed that a large, profitable insured has requested a payment plan for its renewal premium. The insured would like several options to consider. What is the one attribute all of the options must have to protect the insurer?

2. An insurer has a reinsurance recoverable from a reinsurer that is 100 days overdue. The reinsurer has collateralized the reinsurance recoverable with an NAIC approved letter of credit. What, if any, is the penalty for this past due recoverable, and how can it be avoided?

3. KJW Insurance Company receives an average of 200 premium checks per day. The average check is $2,000. It currently takes four days from the time a check is received to the time it is credited to KJW's bank account. KJW management believes that, with the implementation of cash management tools, the time from receipt to crediting can be reduced to two days. Assuming a 5.5 percent interest rate, what is the annual benefit of the reduction in availability float?

4. A financial manager is considering consolidating all of the company's banking needs and dealing with one bank. Doing this would make the company more important to the bank, lower the company's overall banking fees, and simplify managing the banking relationship. What, if any, disadvantages should the financial manager consider before implementing this approach?

Answers to Assignment 5 Questions

NOTE: These answers are provided to give students a basic understanding of acceptable types of responses. They often are not the only valid answers and are not intended to provide an exhaustive response to the questions.

Review Questions

1. The objective of working capital management is to ensure that a company has the resources needed to meet its day-to-day operational requirements and to take advantage of business opportunities that arise.

2. Assets that are considered current for the purposes of assessing working capital, regardless of the nature of the organization, include the following:
   - Cash
   - Marketable securities
   - Accounts receivable

3. A financial manager typically makes the following types of decisions when managing current assets:
   - Whether the company should sell on credit
   - Credit terms that will be offered
   - To whom credit will be extended

4. A credit policy consists of guidelines for determining when credit is to be extended and types of installment plans that will be offered. Insurers implement a credit policy to minimize the incidence of noncollection of premiums.

5. The following tools are used in applying a credit policy:
   a. Credit scoring—Values or weights are assigned to certain credit-related characteristics that, when added together, result in a score of creditworthiness. Typical characteristics used include years in current job, home ownership, payment history, income, and assets.
   b. Credit analysis—The process of evaluating credit information about an individual or organization in order to direct a credit decision. Credit analysis tools available to financial managers and underwriters include financial statements, business credit rating services, and consumer credit reporting agencies.

6. A credit score is calculated in the following way using a simple credit-scoring model:
   - Ascertain a score for each characteristic
   - Calculate a weighted score by multiplying the score and the weight for all characteristics
   - Total all weighted scores
   - Compare weighted total with the credit standard

7. The Z-score model is based on an equation that uses five different financial ratios calculated with information contained in income statements and balance sheets. It is useful in predicting potential bankruptcy for industrial corporations.

8. Credit analysis tools that might be useful to financial managers and underwriters when evaluating an individual or organization include:
   - Financial statements—Useful in identifying and assessing loss exposures, providing data for financial and credit analysis, and providing data for credit-scoring models
   - Business credit rating services—Designed to facilitate financial analysis and help those less skilled in financial analysis to make credit decisions
   - Consumer credit reporting agencies—Useful for assessing applicants' ability to pay premiums and for determining moral-hazard incentives
9. An organization might decide to extend credit to increase sales and to generate additional income.
10. The five "C"s of credit are often used in the credit decision-making process:
    (1) Character—Customer's desire to pay debts
    (2) Capacity—Ability of the customer to pay debts
    (3) Conditions—General economic conditions
    (4) Capital— Customer's financial strength
    (5) Collateral—Assets pledged by the customer against the debt
11. The following issues should be considered when making credit decisions:
    a. Policyholders
       - Federal and state laws applicable to financing
       - Opportunity to earn additional income through service charges
       - Effect on investment income
       - Ability to protect against default in premium payment
       - Character and financial strength of the policyholder
    b. Agents and brokers
       - Creditworthiness of the producer
       - Ability of the producer to collect premiums in a timely manner
       - Reliability of the producer to remit premiums to the insurer in a timely manner
    c. Reinsurers
       - Reinsurer's current financial information
       - Reinsurer's practices and experience with retrocession
       - Reinsurer's general business reputation
       - Status of reinsurer's authorization to transact reinsurance within the primary insurer's state of domicile
       - Need for and adequacy of collateral
       - Reinsurer's financial ratings, state insurance department examinations, loss reserves certifications

12. Producers use the following three primary billing plans:
    (1) Account current billing—The producer pays the insurer the premiums due according to a billing statement prepared by the producer. This plan offers producers the greatest flexibility; however, it presents the highest risk to the insurer.
    (2) Statement billing—Producer pays the insurer according to a statement of policies issued that is sent by the insurer.
    (3) Item billing—Producer accounts to the insurer for each policy individually. More expensive to administer but less risk from a credit decision perspective.
13. Regulators are concerned with reporting requirements regarding reinsurance recoverables because they represent a significant percentage of policyholders' surplus and could affect insurer solvency.
14. The following short-term marketable securities are considered cash equivalents in cash management:
    - Certificates of deposit
    - Commercial paper
    - Repurchase agreements
    - Treasury bills
15. Cash management includes managing day-to-day cash inflows and outflows, forecasting, budgeting, and banking relations.
16. Companies hold some of their assets in the form of cash for the following reasons:
    - To meet transaction needs of day-to-day operations. The amount of cash needed varies based on the size of the transactions and the company's normal operating cycle.
    - To meet precautionary needs, for which cash is required as a financial reserve in case current cash needs exceed the current cash balance.
    - To meet speculative needs, for which management determines the amount of cash the company must have to take advantage of investment and purchase opportunities.
17. The cash operating cycle for a noninsurer typically begins with the initial investment of cash in the production of the company's products and ends with the receipt of cash in the sale of those products. The cash operating cycle for an insurer is in reverse; it begins when the insurer receives the premiums and ends when the insurer pays claims.
18. The following activities help track and control the flow of funds through a company:
    a. Managing float—Companies attempt to shorten cash inflows and lengthen cash outflows to maximize the cash resources available.
    b. Accelerating collections—Companies try to realize the best cash position on a daily basis by managing cash inflows.
    c. Controlling disbursements—Companies minimize the amount of cash held for transaction needs by slowing down disbursements, which increases cash available for short-term investing.
19. The components of availability float are processing float and clearing float. The components of disbursement float are mail float, processing float, and clearing float.

20. The following methods are used to accelerate fund collections:
    - Lockboxes—The collection and immediate deposit of accounts receivable increases the availability of funds through float reduction.
    - Wire transfers—Provide the fastest way to electronically send or receive funds on a same-day basis, and eliminate availability float.
    - Pre-authorized checks—Checks are written on a customer's behalf and are drawn from the customer's checking account.
    - Automated Clearinghouse (ACH) transactions—Pre-authorized electronic debits to checking accounts that typically provide for next-day settlement.

21. The following accounts provide a way of avoiding the possibility of overdrafts:
    - Concentration account—A central account into which funds collected from all sources are transferred.
    - Zero-balance account—A disbursement account into which a transfer of funds from a concentration account is automatically made each day to cover all daily transactions. This eliminates the possibility of overdrafts as long as the concentration account is properly funded.

22. A financial manager is likely to use quality, service, and price as criteria in selecting a bank for cash management purposes.

23. The most important cash management service criteria a financial manager considers in selecting a bank include the following:
    - Strong regional presence
    - Willingness to customize services
    - Expertise of cash management specialists
    - Responsiveness to customer needs
    - Competitive pricing
    - History of freedom from operating errors
    - Superior data processing technology
    - Knowledge of the insurance business

24. Payment methods for bank service activities include the following:
    - Granting earnings allowances on compensating balances
    - Requiring a separate payment for the fees
    - Combination of the preceding two methods

Application Questions

1. To protect itself, the company should structure any of the payment plans being offered to always have enough unearned premium in the policy to serve as collateral if the policyholder should default on any subsequent payments.

2. The penalty for past due reinsurance recoverables is a reduction of policyholder surplus by 20 percent of reinsurance recoverables past due more than ninety days. Although this recoverable is collateralized by an NAIC approved letter of credit, unless the insurer exercises its right to the collateral and eliminates the overdue balance, the penalty applies.

3. The annual benefit of the float is calculated as follows:

Average number of checks received per day	200
Average amount per check	$2,000
Total cash received per day (200 × $2,000)	$400,000
Reduction in availability float time (days)	2
Increase in daily cash balance ($400,000 × 2)	$800,000
Daily value of float ($800,000 × (0.055 ÷ 365))	$120.55
Annual value of float ($120.55 × 365)	$44,001

4. Financial stability and access to adequate lines of credit are particularly important to companies. Bank deposits insured by the FDIC are limited to $100,000, and a line of credit at a failed bank is of no value to a company that needs funds. Companies are often served best by having several different banking relationships with different lines of credit, provided that the cost of maintaining these relationships is not prohibitive.

Direct Your Learning

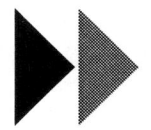

ASSIGNMENT 6

Time Value of Money

Educational Objectives

After learning the content of this assignment, you should be able to:

1. Calculate the future value of a single payment over a single period or over multiple periods, given the applicable interest rate and number of periods.

2. Calculate effective annual interest rates, given stated interest rates and the compounding periods.

3. Calculate the present value of a single future payment over a single period or over multiple periods, given the applicable discount rate and number of periods.

4. Describe the relationship between present value and future value.

5. Calculate the expected rate of return of an investment, given the applicable data.

6. Given the applicable data, use interpolation to determine the discount or interest rate for a factor not listed on a present or future value table.

7. Calculate the number of compounding or discounting periods for an investment, given appropriate variables.

Study Materials

Required Reading:
- Finance for Risk Management and Insurance Professionals
  - Chapter 6

Study Aids:
- SMART Online Practice Exams
- SMART Study Aids
  - Review Notes and Flash Cards—Assignment 6

Outline

- **Future Value and Compounding**
    - A. Future Value Over a Single Period
    - B. Future Value Over Multiple Periods
    - C. Effects of Compounding
- **Present Value and Discounting**
    - A. Present Value Over a Single Period
    - B. Present Value Over Multiple Periods
    - C. Relationship Between Present Value and Future Value
- **Rate of Return and Number of Periods**
    - A. Determining Rates of Return
    - B. Determining Number of Periods
- **Additional Methods of Calculating the Time Value of Money**
    - A. Financial Calculators
    - B. Computer Spreadsheets
    - C. Rule of 72
- **Summary**

s.m.a.r.t. tips — When you take the randomized full practice exams in the SMART Online Practice Exams product, you are using the same software you will use when you take the actual exam. Take advantage of your time and learn the features of the software now.

Key Words and Phrases

Define or describe each of the words and phrases listed below.

Future value (p. 6.4)

Simple interest (p. 6.4)

Compound interest (p. 6.4)

Stated interest rate (p. 6.9)

Effective annual interest rate (p. 6.9)

Present value (p. 6.11)

Discounting (p. 6.11)

Discount rate (p. 6.11)

Review Questions

1. Identify the information needed to calculate an investment's future value for the following periods:

    a. Any single period (p. 6.3)

    Amount of Money Deposited
    Applicable Interest Rate
    Length of Time the Money is Left in the Account

    b. Multiple periods (p. 6.3)

    a.
    + *Method of interest calculation (principel or principal + earned interest)*

2. List the types of rates typically used to calculate the future value of money. (p. 6.4)

    Interest Rates
    Inflation Rates
    Capital Rates of Return

3. Explain how compound interest differs from simple interest. (p. 6.4)

4. Explain why compound interest paid more than once a year produces a higher return than compound interest paid annually. (p. 6.9)

5. Identify the information needed to calculate an investment's present value. (p. 6.11)

   Future Value
   Rate of Growth (and whether compounded or not)
   Number of Periods for which the amount can be invested

6. Explain how the calculation for discounting differs from that for compounding. (p. 6.11)

   Discounting is the process of calculating the present value of a future amount. It is the opposite of compounding.

7. Describe methods used to determine present value calculations. (p. 6.11–6.13, 6.17–6.19)

   $PV = FV_n \div (1 + r)^n$
   Present Value Table
   Financial Calculator

8. Identify the four steps used when interpolating a future value factor. (pp. 6.15–6.16)

9. Describe the usefulness of each of the following methods of calculating the time value of money:
   a. Financial calculators (p. 6.17–6.18)

b. Computer spreadsheets (p. 6.18)

c. Rule of 72 (p. 6.19)

10. List the financial calculator keys helpful in performing time value of money calculations. (p. 6.17)

11. Explain how to estimate the time value of money using the Rule of 72. (p. 6.19)

Application Questions

1. ABC Bank pays 4 percent simple interest on its savings account balances, whereas XYZ Bank pays 4 percent interest compounded annually. If you made a $5,000 deposit in each bank, how much more money would you earn from your XYZ account at the end of ten years?

   ABC = 5,000 + (5000 * .04 * 10)
       = 7,000

   XYZ = FV = PV * (1+r)ⁿ
        5000(1+.04)¹⁰
        5,000 * 1.48
        7,401.22

   7401.22 − 7000.00 = 401.22

2. For each of the following, compute the effective annual interest rates.

Stated Interest Rate (r)	Number of times per year interest is paid (m)	Effective Annual Interest Rate (EAR)
4%	2	2a. 4.04%
4%	4	2b. 4.06%
4%	6	2c. 4.067% 4.07%
4%	12	2d. 4.074% 4.07%

   EAR = (1 + (r/m))^m − 1

3. For each of the following, compute the future value.

Present Value (PV)	Years (N)	Interest Rate (%i)	Future Value (FV)
2,250	10	4%	3a. 3330.58
9,310	8	6%	3b. 14,838.73
76,355	7	8%	3c. 130,859.05
183,796	4	10%	3d. 269,085.72

   FV = PV * (1+r)ⁿ

4. For each of the following, compute the present value.

Present Value (PV)	Years (N)	Interest Rate (%i)	Future Value (FV)
4a. 12,211.33	6	4%	15,451
4b. 30,516.13	9	6%	51,557
4c. 578,506.71	5	8%	850,000
4d. 454,680.99	2	10%	550,164

1.2653
1.6895
1.4693
1.2100

$$PV = FV \div [(1+r)]^n$$

5. For each of the following, solve for the unknown interest rate.

Present Value (PV)	Years (N)	Interest Rate (%i)	Future Value (FV)
500	1	5a. 8%	540
1000	2	5b. 6%	1123.60
1500	3	5c. 10%	1996.50
2000	3	5d. 4%	2249.8

$$FV = PV * (1+r)^n$$
$$(1+r)^n = FV \div PV$$
$$(1+r) = \text{nth root}(FV/PV)$$
$$r = \text{nth root}(FV/PV) - 1$$
$$r = \text{1st root}(540/500) - 1$$
$$r = (540/500) - 1$$
$$r = 1.08 - 1$$
$$r = .08 \text{ or } 8\%$$

6. For each of the following, solve for the unknown number of years.

Present Value (PV)	Years (N)	Interest Rate (%i)	Future Value (FV)
500	6a. 5	4%	608.33
1000	6b. 9	6%	1689.48
1500	6c. 2	8%	1749.60
2000	6d. 10	10%	5187.48

$FV = PV * (1+r)^n$

7. Using interpolation, determine the present value factor for 8.75% in year 9.

$FV = PV * (1+r)^n$

2.1275 rounded 2.13

PV Factor = PV/FV
= 1/2.13
= .4695 or .47

8. A college student was seriously injured by a defective product. The manufacturer of the product is offering the student $270,000 to settle the claim today. The student's lawyer has told her that if she goes to trial she will win $400,000 in the case, but that the case could take 3 years. What is the annual rate of return the student would have to earn on the $270,000 settlement to have it be equal to receiving the $400,000 in four years?

13.998 or 14%

$FV = PV * (1+r)^n$

Answers to Assignment 6 Questions

NOTE: These answers are provided to give students a basic understanding of acceptable types of responses. They often are not the only valid answers and are not intended to provide an exhaustive response to the questions.

Review Questions

1. The information needed to calculate an investment's future value includes the following:
   a. Single period
      - Amount of money deposited
      - Applicable interest rate
      - Length of time the money is left in the account
   b. Multiple periods
      - Amount of money deposited
      - Applicable interest rate
      - Length of time the money is left in the account
      - Method of interest calculation (whether based on principal or principal plus earned interest)

2. Rates used to calculate the future value of money might include interest rates, inflation rates, or capital rates of return.

3. Compound interest earns interest on the original amount invested plus previously earned interest, whereas simple interest earns interest only on the original amount invested.

4. Compound interest paid more than once a year produces a higher return than compound interest paid annually because the interest is earned more often. The more often interest is earned, the more quickly the principal on which the interest is calculated increases.

5. The following information is needed to calculate the present value of an investment:
   - Future value
   - Rate of growth (and whether compounded or not)
   - Number of periods for which the amount can be invested

6. Discounting is the process of calculating the present value of a future amount. It is the opposite of compounding.

7. The following methods might be used to determine the present value of a future amount:
   - Calculate the present value using the following formula:
     $$PV = FV_n \div (1+r)^n.$$
   - Multiply the future value by the present value factor found in the present value table, which shows the present value factors for several combinations of r (interest rate) and n (time period).
   - Using financial calculators or computer spreadsheets

8. The following four steps are used when interpolating a future value factor using a future value table:
   (1) In the row for the appropriate number of periods, find the two interest rates, and the future value factors for those rates, between which the calculated future value factor falls. Calculate the difference between the two factors from the future value table and the difference between the lower table factor and the calculated factor.
   (2) Calculate the percentage of the difference between the factors for the interest rates selected in Step 1 by dividing the difference between the table factor and the calculated factor by the difference between the two table factors.
   (3) Multiply the difference between the interest rates selected in Step 1 by the percentage calculated in Step 2.
   (4) Add the amount calculated in Step 3 to the lower discount rate selected in Step 1 to arrive at the discount rate.

9. The following are useful methods of calculating the time value of money:
   a. Financial calculators—Useful for performing a limited number of time value of money calculations. The user enters three of the four elements of the present value or future value formula and then calculates the present value.
   b. Computer spreadsheets—Useful when significant numbers of calculations are required.
   c. Rule of 72—Useful for quick estimations of the time value of money.

10. Financial calculator keys helpful in performing time value of money calculations include:
    - N (number of periods)
    - %i (interest rate, rate of return, or discount rate per period) (I/Y on the BA II Plus)
    - PV (present value)
    - FV (future value)
    - PMT (payment)
    - CPT (compute)

    Warning: Financial calculator key names will vary based on type of calculator used.

11. The Rule of 72 states that the number of years required for money to double, at a given interest rate and compounded annually, is equal to 72 divided by the interest or discount rate. It is reasonably accurate with interest rates lower than 20 percent.

Application Questions

1. Answer = account balance on XYZ's account at the end of 10 years − account balance on ABC's account at the end of 10 years.

   Account Balance on ABC's account at the end of 10 years:
   Simple interest (formula not provided on the national exam)
   = principal + (principal * interest rate * # of years)
   = 5,000 + (5,000 * .04 * 10)
   = 5,000 + 2,000
   = 7,000

   Account Balance on XYZ's account at the end of 10 years can be calculated in one of three ways:
   a. Using the appropriate tables
   b. Using a financial calculator
   c. Using the formula

   a. Using the appropriate table:

Future Value of $1 at the end of n periods = $(1+r)^n$			
(table provided on national exam)			
FV = 5,000* FV factor(r = 4%, n = 10 years)			
No. of Periods	3%	4%	5%
10	1.3439	1.4802	1.6289

   FV = 5,000 * 1.4802
   FV = 7,401.00

   b. Using the BA II Plus Financial Calculator:
   (be sure that your P/Y = 1)
   Values needed to calculate future value:
   PV = −5,000 (You are depositing the money, it is negative to represent a cash outflow by you)
   PMT = 0.00
   I/Y = 4
   N = 10
   FV = ?

Keystrokes:

| 5000 | +/− | PV |

PV = −5,000

| 0 | PMT |

PMT = 0.00

| 4 | I/Y |

I/Y = 4

| 10 | N |

N = 10

| CPT | FV |

FV = 7,401.22

Screenshot:

c. Using the formula:
Future Value over multiple periods (formula provided on national exam):
$FV = PV*(1+r)^n$
$FV = 5,000*(1+.04)^{10}$
$FV = 5,000*1.48$ (rounded to 2 decimal places)
$FV = 7,400.00$

Answer to the problem:
$7,401.22 − 7,000 = 401.22$

Note: Each method may yield slightly different results due to rounding error. The financial calculator yields the most accurate answer, but all would be acceptable on the national exam.

2. Effective annual interest rates can be calculated in one of two ways:
   a. Using the formula
   b. Using a financial calculator

   Each way is shown below for 2a.

   a. Using the formula: * For these types of problems, the formula is often the simplest method of solving.

   Effective Interest Rate (formula provided on national exam):
   $EAR = (1+(r/m))^m − 1$
   $EAR = (1+(.04/2))^2 − 1$
   $EAR = (1+.02)^2 − 1$
   $EAR = (1.02)^2 − 1$
   $EAR = 1.0404 − 1$
   $EAR = .0404$ or 4.04%

b. Using the BA II Plus Financial Calculator:

Enter the Interest Conversion Worksheet by choosing 2nd ICONV

Keystrokes: [2ND] [2 (ICONV)]

Screenshot: NOM = 0.00

Values:
Nom = 4
C/Y = 2
EFF = ?

Keystrokes: [4] [ENTER] → Screenshot: NOM = 4

Keystrokes: [↑] [2] [ENTER] → Screenshot: C/Y = 2

Keystrokes: [↑] [CPT] → Screenshot: EFF = 4.04

Answer to the problem:

Stated Interest Rate (r)	Number of times per year interest is paid (m)	Effective Annual Interest Rate (EAR)
4%	2	2a. - 4.04%
4%	4	2b. - 4.06%
4%	6	2c. - 4.07%
4%	12	2d. - 4.07%

3. Future Values for various present values, number of years, and interest rates can be calculated in one of three ways:
   a. Using the appropriate tables
   b. Using a financial calculator
   c. Using the formula

   Each way is shown below for 3a.

   a. Using the appropriate table:

Future Value of $1 at the end of n periods = $(1+r)^n$
(table provided on national exam)

   FV = 2,250 * FV factor(r = 4%, n = 10 years)

No. of Periods	3%	4%	5%
10	1.3439	1.4802	1.6289

   FV = 2,250 * 1.4802
   FV = 3,330.45

b. Using the BA II Plus Financial Calculator:
   (be sure that your P/Y = 1)
   Values needed to calculate future value:
   PV = -2,250 (You are depositing the money, it is negative to represent a cash outflow by you)
   PMT = 0.00
   I/Y = 4
   N = 10
   FV = ?

   Keystrokes:

Input	Key		Screenshot
2250	+/–	PV	PV = −2,250
0	PMT		PMT = 0.00
4	I/Y		I/Y = 4
10	N		N = 10
	CPT	FV	FV = 3,330.55

c. Using the formula:
   Future Value over multiple periods (formula provided on national exam):
   $FV = PV*(1+r)^n$
   $FV = 2{,}250*(1+.04)^{10}$
   FV = 2,250*1.4802 (rounded to 4 decimal places)
   FV = 3,330.45

Answer to the problem:

Present Value (PV)	Years (N)	Interest Rate (%i)	Future Value (FV)
2,250	10	4%	3a. - 3,330.55
9,310	8	6%	3b. - 14,838.73
76,355	7	8%	3c. - 130,859.05
183,796	4	10%	3d. - 269,095.72

Time Value of Money 6.17

4. Present Values for various present values, number of years, and interest rates can be calculated in one of three ways:
   a. Using the appropriate tables
   b. Using a financial calculator
   c. Using the formula

   Each way is shown below for 4a.

   a. Using the appropriate table:

   | Present Value of $1 at the end of n periods = $1/(1+r)^n$ |
   | (table provided on national exam) |

   PV = 15,451* PV factor($r = 4\%$, $n = 6$ years)

No. of Periods	3%	4%	5%
6	0.8375	0.7903	0.7462

   PV = 15,451 * 0.7903
   PV = 12,210.93

   b. Using the BA II Plus Financial Calculator:
   (be sure that your P/Y = 1)
   Values:

   FV = 15,451 (It is positive, assuming you will receive the money at some point in the future, it will represent a cash inflow to you)
   PMT = 0.00
   I/Y = 4
   N = 6
   PV = ?

   Keystrokes:

15451	FV
0	PMT
4	I/Y
6	N
CPT	PV

   Screenshot:

   FV = 15,451
   PMT = 0.00
   I/Y = 4
   N = 6
   PV = −12,211.15

   (You are depositing the money, it is negative to represent a cash outflow by you)

c. Using the formula:
Future Value over multiple periods (formula provided on national exam):
PV = FV / [(1+r)^n]
PV = 15,451 / [(1+.04)^6]
PV = 15,451 / 1.2653 (rounded to 4 decimal places)
PV = 12,211.33

Answer to the problem:

Present Value (PV)	Years (N)	Interest Rate (%i)	Future Value (FV)
4a. - 12,211.15	6	4%	15,451
4b. - 30,516.51	9	6%	51,557
4c. - 578,495.72	5	8%	850,000
4d. - 454,680.99	2	10%	550,164

5. Interest rates for various present values, number of years, and future values can be calculated in one of three ways:
   a. Using the appropriate tables
   b. Using a financial calculator
   c. Using the formula

Each way is shown below for 5a.

a. Using the appropriate table:
Solving for the FV factor:
FV factor(r = ??%, n = 1 year) = FV/PV
FV factor(r = ??%, n = 1 year) = 540/500
FV factor(r = ??%, n = 1 year) = 1.08

Looking across the number of periods = 1 (# of years) row, the factor 1.08 is associated with 8% interest

Future Value of $1 at the end of n Periods = (1+r)^n (table provided on national exam)			
FV = PV* FV factor(r = ??%, n = 1 year)			
No. of Periods	7%	8%	9%
1	1.0700	1.0800	1.0900

Interest Rate = 8%

b. Using the BA II Plus Financial Calculator:
(be sure that your P/Y = 1)
Values:

FV = 540 (It is positive, assuming you will receive the money at some point in the future, it will represent a cash inflow to you)

PMT = 0.00

PV = -500 (You are depositing the money, it is negative to represent a cash outflow by you)

N = 1

I/Y = ?

Keystrokes:

			Screenshot:	
540	FV		FV =	540
0	PMT		PMT =	0.00
500	+/−	PV	PV =	-500
1	N		N =	1
CPT	I/Y			8.00%

c. Using the formula:
Future Value over multiple periods (formula provided on national exam):

$FV = PV*(1+r)^n$

Solve for r:

$(1+r)^n = FV/PV$

$(1+r) = $ nth root (FV/PV)

$r = $ nth root $(FV/PV) - 1$

$r = $ 1st root $(540/500) - 1$

$r = (540/500) - 1$

$r = 1.08 - 1$

$r = .08$ or 8%

Answer to the problem:

Present Value (PV)	Years (N)	Interest Rate (%i)	Future Value (FV)
500	1	5a. - 8%	540
1000	2	5b. - 6%	1123.60
1500	3	5c. -10%	1996.50
2000	3	5d. - 4%	2249.8

6. The number of years for various present values, future values, and interest rates can be calculated in one of three ways:
   a. Using the appropriate tables
   b. Using a financial calculator
   c. Using the formula

   Each way is shown below for 6a.

   a. Using the appropriate table:
      Solving for the FV factor:
      FV factor(r = 4%, n = ?? years)= FV/PV
      FV factor(r = 4%, n = ?? years)= 608.33/500
      FV factor(r = 4%, n = ?? years)= 1.2167

      Looking down the compound interest rate = 4% column, the factor 1.2167 is associated with 5 years

Future Value of $1 at the end of n Periods = $(1+r)^n$			
(table provided on national exam)			
FV = PV* FV factor(r = 4%, n = ?? years)			
No. of Periods	3%	4%	5%
4	1.1255	1.1699	1.2155
5	1.1593	1.2167	1.2763
6	1.1941	1.2653	1.3401

   Answer: # of years = 5

b. Using the BA II Plus Financial Calculator:
(be sure that your P/Y = 1)
Values:
FV = 608.33 (It is positive, assuming you will receive the money at some point in the future, it will represent a cash inflow to you)
PMT = 0.00
PV = -500 (You are depositing the money, it is negative to represent a cash outflow by you)
I/Y = 4.00%
N = ?

Keystrokes: Screenshot:

608.33   [FV]   FV = 608.33

0   [PMT]   PMT = 0.00

500 [+/-] [PV]   PV = -500

4   [I/Y]   I/Y = 4.00%

[CPT] [N]   5.00

c. Using the formula:
Future Value over multiple periods (formula provided on national exam):
$FV = PV*(1+r)^n$
Solve for n:
$(1+r)^n = FV/PV$
Using trial and error.
$(1+.04)^n = 608.33/500$
$1.04^n = 1.21666$
$1.04^4 = 1.1699$ and $1.04^6 = 1.2653$, so it must be somewhere in between:
$1.04^5 = 1.21666$
N = 5

Answer to the problem:

Present Value (PV)	Years (N)	Interest Rate (%i)	Future Value (FV)
500	6a. - 5	4%	608.33
1000	6b. - 9	6%	1689.48
1500	6c. - 2	8%	1749.60
2000	6d. - 10	10%	5187.48

7. Interpolation involves the following four steps:

	Present Value of $1 to be Received After n Periods Table Factor	Discount Interest Rate (%i)	Discount Rate Interpolation
Step 1:	0.5002	8.00%	8.00%
			8.75%
	0.4241	10.00%	
Differences	-.0761	2.00	.75

Step 2: .75/2.00 = 0.375

Step 3: -.0761*0.375 = -0.02854

Step 4: 0.5002 – 0.02854 = .4717

This answer can be verified using a financial calculator:

Using the BA II Plus Financial Calculator:

(be sure that your P/Y = 1)

Values:

PV = -1 (You are depositing the money, it is negative to represent a cash outflow by you)

PMT = 0.00

I/Y = 8.75

N = 9

FV = ?

Keystrokes: Screenshot:

1	+/–	PV	PV = -1
0		PMT	PMT = 0.00
8.75		I/Y	I/Y = 8.75
9		N	N = 9
	CPT	FV	FV = 2.13

Then the PV factor(r=8.75, n=9) = PV/FV
PV factor(r=8.75, n=9) = 1/2.13
PV factor(r=8.75, n=9) = .47

The difference between the interpolation answer and the calculator answer (almost .002) shows how inaccurate interpolation can be.

8. Similar to application question 5, the annual rate or return (interest rates) for various present values, number of years, and future values can be calculated in one of three ways:
   a. Using the appropriate tables
   b. Using a financial calculator
   c. Using the formula

   a. Using the appropriate table:
      Solving for the FV factor:
      FV factor(r = ??%, n = 3 years) = FV/PV
      FV factor(r = ??%, n = 3 years) = 400,000/270,000
      FV factor(r = ??%, n = 3 years) = 1.4815
      Looking across the number of periods = 3 (# of years) row, the factor 1.4815 is 14%.

Future Value of $1 at the end of n Periods = $(1+r)^n$			
(table provided on national exam)			
FV = PV* FV factor(r = ??%, n = 3 years)			
No. of Periods	12%	14%	16%
3	1.4049	1.4815	1.5609

b. Using the BA II Plus Financial Calculator:
(be sure that your P/Y = 1)
Values:
FV = 400,000 (It is positive, assuming you will receive the money at some point in the future, it will represent a cash inflow to you)
PMT = 0.00
PV = -270,000 (You are depositing the money, it is negative to represent a cash outflow by you)
N = 3
I/Y = ?

Keystrokes: Screenshot:

400000   [FV]   FV =   400,000

0   [PMT]   PMT =   0.00

270000   [+/−]   [PV]   PV =   -270,000

3   [N]   N =   3

[CPT]   [I/Y]   14.00%

c. Using the formula:
Future Value over multiple periods (formula provided on national exam):
FV = PV*(1+r)^n
Solve for r:
(1+r)^n = FV/PV
(1+r) = nth root (FV/PV)
r = nth root (FV/PV) − 1
r = 3rd root (400,000/270,000) −1
r = 3rd root (400,000/270,000) − 1 taking the 3rd root is the same as raising a number to the 1/3rd or .333333333 power on a calculator using the y^x button.
r = 1.14 −1
r = 14.00%

Direct Your Learning

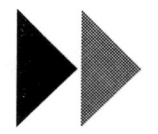

Assignment 7

Discounted Cash Flow Valuation

Educational Objectives

After learning the content of this assignment, you should be able to:

1. Calculate the future and present values of an annuity cash flow, given the applicable interest rate and number of periods.
2. Contrast an annuity due with an ordinary annuity.
3. Calculate the present value of a perpetuity, given applicable information.
4. Calculate the future and present values of uneven cash flows, given the applicable interest rate and number of periods.
5. Calculate periodic loan payments, given the type of loan and applicable interest rate and number of payments.

Study Materials

Required Reading:
- Finance for Risk Management and Insurance Professionals
  - Chapter 7

Study Aids:
- SMART Online Practice Exams
- SMART Study Aids
  - Review Notes and Flash Cards—Assignment 7

Outline

- **Annuity Valuation**
    A. Future Value of an Ordinary Annuity
    B. Present Value of an Ordinary Annuity
    C. Annuities Due
    D. Perpetuities
- **Future and Present Values of Unequal Cash Flows**
    A. Future Value of a Stream of Unequal Payments
    B. Present Value of a Stream of Unequal Payments
- **Additional Methods of Discounted Cash Flow Calculation**
    A. Financial Calculators
    B. Computer Spreadsheets
    C. Interpolation
- **Types of Loans**
    A. Pure Discount Loans
    B. Interest-Only Loans
    C. Amortized Loans
- **Summary**

Set aside a specific, realistic amount of time to study every day.

Key Words and Phrases
Define or describe each of the words and phrases listed below.

Annuity (p. 7.3)

Ordinary annuity (p. 7.4)

Annuity due (p. 7.10)

Perpetuity (p. 7.12)

Pure discount loan (p. 7.22)

Interest-only loan (p. 7.23)

Amortized loan (p. 7.23)

Balloon loan (p. 7.24)

Review Questions

1. Describe the three common types of annuities. (pp. 7.4–7.12)

2. Identify the information needed to compute the future value of an ordinary annuity. (p. 7.4)

3. Describe the methods of determining the future value of an ordinary annuity. (pp. 7.4–7.5, 7.19)

4. Illustrate how the future value of an annuity formula can be used to determine the period payment. (p. 7.5)

5. Describe how to calculate the present value of a series of cash flows. (p. 7.7)

6. Identify the factor that results in the difference in the present value calculations for an annuity due and an ordinary annuity. (pp. 7.10–7.11)

7. Explain why an understanding of discounted cash flow valuation is important. (p. 7.21)

8. Identify the two activities involved in all loans. (p. 7.21)

9. Explain how to use discounted cash flow methods to calculate the present or future value of loan amounts. (p. 7.22)

10. Describe the following types of loans:
    a. Pure discount loan (pp. 7.22–7.23)

b. Interest-only loan (p. 7.23)

c. Amortized loan (pp. 7.23–7.24)

11. Explain how a loan is amortized. (pp. 7.23–7.24)

Application Questions

1. ABC Company has identified an investment project with the following cash flows paid at the end of each year. If the discount rate is 10 percent, what is the present value of these cash flows?

Year	Cash Flow
1	$1,300
2	500
3	700
4	1,620

2. Investment X offers to pay $3,000 per year for eight years, whereas Investment Y offers to pay $5,000 per year for four years. For both investments, payments are made at the end of each year. Which of these cash flow streams has the higher present value if the discount rate is 6 percent?

3. A company has identified an investment project with the cash flows shown in the following table. If the discount rate is 8 percent, what is the future value of these cash flows at the end of Year 4? (Assume that the cash flows occur at the end of the year.)

Year	Cash Flow
1	$ 900
2	1,000
3	1,100
4	1,200

4. An investment offers $4,100 per year for ten years, with the first payment occurring one year from now. If the required return is 10 percent, what is the present value of the investment?

5. If $20,000 is put up today in exchange for an 8 percent, nine-year annuity beginning one year from now, what will the annual cash flow be?

6. A company will generate an annual $75,000 expense reduction each year for the next eight years from a new information database. The computer system needed to set up the database costs $420,000. If the company can borrow the money to buy the computer system at 8 percent annual interest, is it worth the investment?

7. If $1,500 is deposited at the end of each of the next ten years into an account paying 6 percent interest, how much money will be in the account at the end of ten years?

8. XYZ, Inc., wants to have $50,000 in its savings account five years from now and is prepared to make equal annual deposits into the account at the end of each year. If the account pays 6 percent interest, what amount must XYZ deposit each year?

9. ABC Bank offers a $35,000, seven-year term loan at 10 percent annual interest. (Payments made annually at the end of the year.) What will the annual loan payment be?

Answers to Assignment 7 Questions

NOTE: These answers are provided to give students a basic understanding of acceptable types of responses. They often are not the only valid answers and are not intended to provide an exhaustive response to the questions.

Review Questions

1. The following are the three common types of annuities:
   (1) A series of equal periodic payments made at the end of each period for a specific period of time. This type of annuity is called an ordinary annuity.
   (2) A series of equal periodic payments made at the beginning of each period for a specific period of time. This type of annuity is called an annuity due.
   (3) A series of fixed payments made on specified dates over an indefinite period. This type of annuity is called a perpetuity.

2. The information needed to compute the future value of an ordinary annuity includes the payment amount, the number of intervals over which the annuity is paid, and the interest rate at which payments can earn interest.

3. The following methods can be used to determine the future value of an ordinary annuity:
   (1) Calculate the future value of each individual payment $FV = PV \times (1+r)^n$ and then sum the future values calculated. This can also be expressed as $FVA = A \times [(1+r)^{n-1} + (1+r)^{n-2} +...+ (1+r)^{n-n}]$.
   (2) Use a future value table: Multiply the payment per period by the table value in the r interest rate column at the n period row $FVA = A \times FVAF$.
   (3) Use a financial calculator or spreadsheet

4. The future value of an annuity formula, $FVA = A \times [((1+r)^n - 1) \div r]$, can be rearranged as follows to determine the period payment: $A = FVA \div [((1+r)^n - 1) \div r]$.

5. To calculate the present value of a series of cash flows, calculate the present value of each individual payment and then sum the present values calculated, if the cash flows are equal value using the following formula:
$$PVA = A \times [(1 \div (1+r)) + (1 \div (1+r)^2) +...+ (1 \div (1+r)^n)].$$

6. The difference between the calculation of the present value of an annuity due and an ordinary annuity is caused by the differing number of earning periods. An ordinary annuity has one less earning period because of the additional earning period of an annuity due created by receiving payments at the beginning of the period rather than at the end.

7. An understanding of discounted cash flow valuation is important because many business decisions involve multiple cash inflows and outflows over a period of many years. Having a knowledge of discounted cash flow valuation enables an organization to value loans and assess the different forms of repayment of principal and interest.

8. The two activities involved in all loans include:
   (1) An amount of money is provided to the borrower by the lender.
   (2) The loaned amount, plus interest, must be repaid by the borrower to the lender by a specific date.

9. Discounted cash flow methods can be used to calculate the present or future value of loan amounts by using the following values in the future and present value formulas:
   - Loan repayments are the periodic payments.
   - Loan duration is the number of years or periods.
   - Interest rate charged is either the interest or discount rate.
10. The following are common types of loans:
    a. Pure discount loans are loans that provide a lump sum of money to a borrower today and are repaid with interest by payment of a single lump sum at a specific future date. These loans are generally used for loan periods of less than one year. In effect, the borrower receives the present value of the amount to be repaid.
    b. Interest-only loans are loans that require the borrower to make only interest payments on a periodic basis during the life of the loan and to repay the original amount of the loan on a specified future date. These loans are usually available for short- to medium-term financing.
    c. Amortized loans are loans that require the borrower to make payments consisting of both principal and interest over the duration of the loan, which will cause the loan to be completely repaid at the end of a specified time period.
11. A loan is amortized by making variable periodic payments equal to a fixed periodic loan repayment plus the interest due, or by making a fixed total payment and allocating the payment between loan repayment and interest.

Application Questions

1. The present value of an uneven series of cash flows can be calculated in one of two ways:
   a. Using the appropriate tables
   b. Using the formula

   a. Using the appropriate table:

Present Value of $1 at the end of n periods = $1/(1+r)^n$ (table provided on national exam)	
No. of Periods	10%
1	0.9091
2	0.8264
3	0.7513
4	0.6830

   PV of Year 1 CF:
   $\quad$ PV = 1,300* PV factor(r = 10%, n = 1 year)
   $\quad$ PV = 1,300 * 0.9091
   $\quad$ PV = 1181.83

   PV of Year 2 CF:
   $\quad$ PV = 500* PV factor(r = 10%, n = 2 years)
   $\quad$ PV = 500 * 0.8264
   $\quad$ PV = 413.20

PV of Year 3 CF:
    PV = 700* PV factor(r = 10%, n = 3 years)
    PV = 700 * 0.7513
    PV = 525.91

PV of Year 4 CF:
    PV = 1,620* PV factor(r = 10%, n = 4 years)
    PV = 1,620 * 0.6830
    PV = 1106.46

Answer = sum of all four present values:
1181.83 + 413.20 + 525.91 + 1106.46 = 3227.40

  b. Using the formula:

The present value of the cash flow is: $PV = FV \div (1+r)^n$

$\$1{,}300 \div 1.1 = \$1{,}181.82$

$\$500 \div 1.1^2 = \$413.22$

$\$700 \div 1.1^3 = \$525.92$

$\$1{,}620 \div 1.1^4 = \$1{,}106.48$

Total = $3,227.44 (sum the calculated PVs)

2. The present value of a series of even cash flows, known as the present value of an ordinary annuity can be calculated in one of three ways:

  a. Using the appropriate tables
  b. Using a financial calculator
  c. Using the formula

  a. Using the appropriate table:

| Present Value of an annuity of $1 per period for n periods = $[1-(1/(1+r)^n)]/r$ ||
| (table provided on national exam) ||
No. of Periods	6%
1	0.9434
2	1.8334
3	2.6730
4	3.4651
5	4.2124
6	4.9173
7	5.5824
8	6.2098

Investment X:
  PV of Investment X:
  PV = 3,000* PVA factor(r = 6%, n = 8 years)
  PV = 3,000 * 6.2098
  PV = 18,629.40

Investment Y:
  PV of Investment Y:
  PV = 5,000* PVA factor(r = 6%, n = 4 years)
  PV = 5,000 * 3.4651
  PV = 17,325.50

Therefore Investment X has the highest present value of future cash flows.

b. Using the BA II Plus Financial Calculator:
   (be sure that your P/Y = 1)
   Investment X:
   Values:
   FV = 0
   PMT = 3,000.00
   I/Y = 6
   N = 8
   PV = -18,629.38 (Present value is shown as a negative number to represent how much you would have to invest today (cash outflow) to receive the 3,000 per year for the next 8 years).

   Keystrokes: Screenshot:

0	FV		FV = 0
3000.00	PMT		PMT = 3,000.00
6	I/Y		I/Y = 6
8	N		N = 8
CPT	PV		PV = -18,629.38

Investment Y:
   Values:
   FV = 0
   PMT = 5,000.00
   I/Y = 6
   N = 4
   PV = -17,325.53 (Present value is shown as a negative number to represent how much you would have to invest today (cash outflow) to receive the 5,000 per year for the next 4 years).

   Keystrokes: Screenshot:

Keystroke	Button		Screen
0	FV		FV = 0
5000.00	PMT		PMT = 5,000.00
6	I/Y		I/Y = 4
4	N		N = 8
CPT	PV		PV = -17,325.53

   Therefore Investment X has the highest present value of future cash flows.

c. **Using the formula:**
   Calculated using the formula: $PVA = A \times [(1 \div (1+r)) + (1 \div (1+r)^2) + ... + (1 \div (1+r)^n)]$.
   Present value Investment X = $3,000 × [(1 ÷ 1.06) + (1 ÷ 1.06²) +...+ (1 ÷ 1.06⁸)]
       = $3,000 × 6.209794
       = $18,629.38
   Present value Investment Y = $5,000 × [(1 ÷ 1.06) + (1 ÷ 1.06²) +...+ (1 ÷ 1.06⁴)]
       = $5,000 × 3.465106
       = $17,325.53.

   Therefore, the Investment X is more valuable than the Investment Y.

3. The future value of an uneven series of cash flows can be calculated in one of two ways:
   a. Using the appropriate tables
   b. Using the formula
   a. Using the appropriate table:

Future Value of $1 at the end of n periods = $(1+r)^n$ (table provided on national exam)	
No. of Periods	8%
1	1.08
2	1.1664
3	1.2597
4	1.3605

   PV of Year 1 CF:

   FV = 900* FV factor(r = 8%, n = 3 years) Three years is the amount of time from the time of the payment of the cash flow for year 1 (paid at the end of year 1) until the time the future value is being calculated (end of year 4).

   FV = 900* 1.2597

   FV = 1,133.73

   FV of Year 2 CF:

   FV = 1,000* FV factor(r = 8%, n = 2 years)

   FV = 1,000 * 1.1664

   FV = 1,166.40

   FV of Year 3 CF:

   FV = 1,100* FV factor(r = 8%, n = 1 year)

   FV = 1,100 * 1.08

   FV = 1,188

   FV of Year 4 CF:

   FV = 1,200 Year 4 cash flow is paid at the same time as the time the future value is being calculated (end of year 4).

   Answer = sum of all four present values:

   1133.73 + 1,166.40 + 1,188 + 1,200 = $4688.13

b. Using the formula:

The future value of the cash flows is calculated using the formula $FV = PV \times (1+r)^n$, then summing the future values.

$900 \times 1.08^3 = \$1,133.74$

$1,000 \times 1.08^2 = \$1,166.40$

$1,100 \times 1.08^1 = \$1,188.00$

$1,200 \times 1.08^0 = \$1,200.00$

Total = $4,688.14

4. The present value of a series of even cash flows, known as the present value of an ordinary annuity can be calculated in one of three ways:
   a. Using the appropriate tables
   b. Using a financial calculator
   c. Using the formula

   a. Using the appropriate table:

Present Value of an annuity of $1 per period for n periods = $[1-(1/(1+r)^n)]/r$	
(table provided on national exam)	
No. of Periods	10%
1	0.9091
2	1.7355
3	2.4869
4	3.1699
5	3.7908
6	4.3553
7	4.8684
8	5.3349
9	5.7590
10	6.1446

Investment X:

PV of Investment:

PV = 4,100 * PVA factor(r = 10%, n = 10 years)

PV = 4,100 * 6.1446

PV = 25,192.86

b. Using the BA II Plus Financial Calculator:
    (be sure that your P/Y = 1)
    Values:
    FV = 0
    PMT = 4,100.00
    I/Y = 10
    N = 10
    CPT – PV = -25,192.73 (Present value is shown as a negative number to represent how much you would have to invest today (cash outflow) to receive the 4,100 per year for the next 10 years).

    Keystrokes:

    | 0 | FV |
    | 4100.00 | PMT |
    | 10 | I/Y |
    | 10 | N |
    | CPT | PV |

    Screenshot:

    FV = 0
    PMT = 4,100.00
    I/Y = 10
    N = 10
    PV = -25,192.73

c. Using the formula:
    The present value of the investment is calculated using the formula
    $PVA = A \times [(1 \div (1+r)) + (1 \div (1+r)^2) + ... + (1 \div (1+r)^n)]$.
    Present value = $\$4{,}100 \times [(1 \div 1.1) + (1 \div 1.1^2) + ... + (1 \div 1.1^{10})] = \$4{,}100 \times 6.144567 = \$25192.73$.

5. The payment value of a series of even cash flows, known as the present value of an ordinary annuity can be calculated in one of three ways:
   a. Using the appropriate tables
   b. Using a financial calculator
   c. Using the formula
   a. Using the appropriate table:

Present Value of an annuity of $1 per period for n periods = $[1-(1/(1+r)^n)]/r$	
(table provided on national exam)	
No. of Periods	8%
1	0.9259
2	1.7833
3	2.5771
4	3.3121
5	3.9927
6	4.6229
7	5.2064
8	5.7466
9	6.2469
10	6.7101

Annual Cash Flow:
  20,000 = PMT * PVA factor(r = 8%, n = 9 years)
  20,000 = PMT * 6.2469
  PMT = 20,000/6.2469
  PMT = 3,201.59

b. Using the BA II Plus Financial Calculator:
(be sure that your P/Y = 1)
Investment X:
Values:
FV = 0
PV = -20,000 (Present value is shown as a negative number to represent how much you would have to invest today (cash outflow) to receive the cash flow per year for the next 9 years).
I/Y = 8
N = 9
PMT = ?

Keystrokes: Screenshot:

| 0 | FV | | FV = 0 |

| 20000 | +/− | PV | PV = -20,000.00 |

| 8 | I/Y | | I/Y = 8 |

| 9 | N | | N = 9 |

| CPT | PMT | | PMT = 3,201.59 |

c. Using the formula:
A nine-year annuity of $1 at 8 percent can be computed as follows:
$1 \times (1 \div 1.08 + 1 \div 1.08^2 + ... + 1 \div 1.08^9) = 6.246888$.

The annuity amount times this value must equal $20,000; therefore, dividing $20,000 by 6.246888 yields $3,201.59.

As a check, $3,201.59 × 6.246888 = $20,000, as required.

6. To answer this question, you need to compare the present value of the annual expense reduction to the initial cost of the database, this is commonly known as a net present value calculation. If the present value of future expense reductions are greater than the initial costs, then installing the database is worth undertaking.

The present value of a series of even cash flows, known as the present value of an ordinary annuity can be calculated in one of three ways:

a. Using the appropriate tables
b. Using a financial calculator
c. Using the formula

a. Using the appropriate table:

Present Value of an annuity of $1 per period for n periods = $[1-(1/(1+r)^n)]/r$ (table provided on national exam)	
No. of Periods	8%
1	0.9259
2	1.7833
3	2.5771
4	3.3121
5	3.9927
6	4.6229
7	5.2064
8	5.7466
9	6.2469
10	6.7101

Annual Cash Flow:
PV = 75,000 * PVA factor($r = 8\%, n = 8$ years)
PV = 75,000 * 5.7466
PV = 430,995

Since the present value of the annual reduction in expenses (430,995) is greater than the initial cost (420,000) the net present value (430,995 − 420,000 = 10,995) is positive and installing the database is worthwhile to the company.

b. Using the BA II Plus Financial Calculator:

(be sure that your P/Y = 1)

Database Investment:

Values:

FV = 0

PMT = 75,000

I/Y = 8

N = 8

CPT − PV = -430,997.92 (Present value is shown as a negative number to represent how much you would have to invest today (cash outflow) to receive the cash flow per year for the next 8 years).

Since the present value of the annual reduction in expenses (430,997.92) is greater than the initial cost (420,000) the net present value (430,995 − 420,000 = 10,997.92) is positive and installing the database is worthwhile to the company.

Keystrokes: Screenshot:

0	FV	FV = 0
75000	PMT	PMT = 75,000.00
8	I/Y	I/Y = 8
8	N	N = 8
CPT	PV	PV = -430,997.92

c. Using the formula:

The present value of the annual reduction in expenses is found by solving the equation:

PV = 75,000 × [(1 ÷ 1.08) + (1 ÷ 1.08^2) +...+ (1 ÷ 1.08^8)]

PV = 75,000 × 5.746639 =

PV = $430,997.93.

Because the present value of net income (annual reduction in expenses) exceeds the present value of initial investment (420,000), the loan should be obtained. [Note the assumption that each period's net payment is positive.]

7. This question is asking for the future value of an ordinary annuity.

The future value of a series of even cash flows paid at the end of each time period, known as the future value of an ordinary annuity can be calculated in one of three ways:
a. Using the appropriate tables
b. Using a financial calculator
c. Using the formula

a. Using the appropriate table:

Future Value of an annuity of $1 per period for n periods = $[1-(1/(1+r)^n)]/r$ (table provided on national exam)	
No. of Periods	6%
1	1.0000
2	2.0600
3	3.1836
4	4.3746
5	5.6371
6	6.9753
7	8.3938
8	9.8975
9	11.4913
10	13.1808

Calculate Future Value:

FV = 1,500* FVA factor(r = 6%, n = 10 years)

FV = 1,500 * 13.1808

FV = 19,771.20

b. Using the BA II Plus Financial Calculator:
   (be sure that your P/Y = 1)
   Annual Deposit Future Value calculation:
   Values:
   PV = 0
   PMT = -1,500 (Payment is shown as a negative number to represent how much you would have to invest at the end of each year (cash outflow) to receive the future value at the end of 10 years).
   I/Y = 6
   N = 10
   CPT – FV = 19771.19
   Keystrokes: Screenshot:

   | 0 | PV | PV =   0

   | 1500 | +/– | PMT | PMT = 75,000.00

   | 6 | I/Y | I/Y =   6

   | 10 | N | N =   10

   | CPT | FV | FV =   19,771.19

c. Using the formula:
   The future value of the annual deposit is found by solving the equation:
   FV = $1,500 × (1.06^9 + 1.06^8 +...+ 1.06^0) = $1,500 × 13.18079 = $19,771.19 will be available in ten years.

8. This question is asking for the payment required to generate a specified future value of an ordinary annuity.

The payment needed to generate a specified future value of a series of even cash flows paid at the end of each time period, known as the future value of an ordinary annuity can be calculated in one of three ways:
   a. Using the appropriate tables
   b. Using a financial calculator
   c. Using the formula

   a. Using the appropriate table:

Future Value of an annuity of $1 per period for n periods = $[1-(1/(1+r)^n)]/r$ (table provided on national exam)	
No. of Periods	6%
1	1.0000
2	2.0600
3	3.1836
4	4.3746
5	5.6371
6	6.9753
7	8.3938
8	9.8975
9	11.4913
10	13.1808

Calculate the payment needed:
50,000 = PMT* FVA factor(r = 6%, n = 5 years)
50,000 = PMT * 5.6371
PMT = 50,000/5.6371
PMT = 8869.81

b. Using the BA II Plus Financial Calculator:
(be sure that your P/Y = 1)
Savings Account Deposits:
Values:
PV = 0
FV = 50,000
I/Y = 6
N = 5
CPT – PMT = -8869.82 (Payment is shown as a negative number to represent how much you would have to invest at the end of each year (cash outflow) to receive the future value at the end of 10 years).

Keystrokes:

0	PV
50000	FV
6	I/Y
5	N
CPT	PMT

Screenshot:

PV = 0
FV = 50,000.00
I/Y = 6
N = 5
PMT = -8,869.82

c. Using the formula:
The annual deposit is found by solving the equation:
XYZ must deposit the following amount each year:
FVA = A × [(1+r)^n –1)] ÷ r]
50,000 = Deposit × (1.06^4 + 1.06^3 +...+ 1.06^0)
50,000 = Deposit × 5.637093
Deposit = $50,000 ÷ 5.637093 = $8,869.82.

9. This question is asking for the payment required to generate a specified present value of an ordinary annuity.

The payment needed to generate a specified present value of a series of even cash flows paid at the end of each time period, known as the present value of an ordinary annuity can be calculated in one of three ways:
   a. Using the appropriate tables
   b. Using a financial calculator
   c. Using the formula

a. Using the appropriate table:

Present Value of an annuity of $1 per period for n periods = $[1-(1/(1+r)^n)]/r$ (table provided on national exam)	
No. of Periods	10%
1	0.9091
2	1.7355
3	2.4869
4	3.1699
5	3.7908
6	4.3553
7	4.8684
8	5.3349
9	5.7590
10	6.1446

Calculate the payment needed:

35000 = PMT* PVA factor(r = 10%, n = 7 years)

35,000 = PMT * 4.8684

PMT = 35,000/4.8684

PMT = 7,189.22

b. Using the BA II Plus Financial Calculator:
(be sure that your P/Y = 1)
Loan Payments:
Values:
PV = 35,000
FV = 0
I/Y = 10
N = 7
CPT – PMT = -7,189.19 (Payment is shown as a negative number to represent how much you would have to pay at the end of each year (cash outflow) to receive the present value today).

Keystrokes: Screenshot:

35000   PV   PV =   35,000

0   FV   FV =   0

10   I/Y   I/Y =   10

7   N   N =   7

CPT   PMT   PMT = -7,189.19

c. Using the formula:
The present value of the seven annual payments discounted at 10 percent must equal $35,000.
Therefore:
$35,000 = \text{Payment} \times [(1 \div 1.1) + (1 \div 1.1^2) + \ldots + (1 \div 1.1^7)]$
$35,000 = \text{Payment} \times 4.868419$
Payment = $35,000 \div 4.868419 = \$7,189.19$.

Direct Your Learning

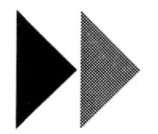

Bonds and Stocks

Educational Objectives

After learning the content of this assignment, you should be able to:

1. Describe the basic components and additional features of bonds.

2. Contrast asset-backed securities, mortgage-backed securities, and debenture bonds.

3. Describe the effects of the following on bond pricing: interest rates, maturity, yield to maturity, inflation, and ratings by nationally recognized statistical rating organizations.

4. Given appropriate data, calculate the current price of a bond.

5. Describe the four classifications of bonds.

6. Explain how the income tax rules for interest paid on municipal bonds affects the interest rates paid on these bonds.

7. Explain how bonds are presented on the financial statements of insurers and noninsurers.

8. Describe the characteristics and methods of pricing common and preferred stock.

9. Describe the effects of the efficient market hypothesis on stock pricing.

10. Given appropriate data, calculate the price of a stock using the dividend growth model.

11. Explain how stocks are presented on the financial statements of insurers and noninsurers.

Study Materials

Required Reading:
- Finance for Risk Management and Insurance Professionals
  - Chapter 8

Study Aids:
- SMART Online Practice Exams
- SMART Study Aids
  - Review Notes and Flash Cards—Assignment 8

Outline

- **Bonds**
  - A. Basic Bond Components
  - B. Additional Bond Features
  - C. Bond Collateral
  - D. Components Affecting Bond Pricing
    1. Interest Rates
    2. Maturity
    3. Yield to Maturity (YTM)
    4. Inflation
    5. Nationally Recognized Statistical Rating Organizations
  - E. Calculating the Price of a Bond
  - F. Classifications of Bonds
    1. Federal Debt
    2. Corporate Bonds
    3. State and Local Debt
    4. International Bonds
  - G. Financial Statement Presentation of Bonds
    1. Bond Valuation Under Statutory Accounting Principles
    2. Bond Valuation Under Generally Accepted Accounting Principles

- **Stocks**
  - A. Stock Characteristics
    1. Preferred Stock
    2. Common Stock
  - B. Stock Pricing
    1. Preferred Stock Pricing
    2. Common Stock Pricing
    3. Reasons for Stock Price Volatility
    4. Fundamental Analysis
    5. Technical Analysis
    6. Efficient Market Hypothesis
    7. Dividend Growth Model
  - C. Financial Statement Presentation of Stocks
    1. Stock Valuation Under Statutory Accounting Principles
    2. Stock Valuation Under Generally Accepted Accounting Principles

- **Summary**

Study tips: Plan to take one week to complete each assignment in your course.

Key Words and Phrases

Define or describe each of the words and phrases listed below.

Bond (p. 8.4)

Indenture agreement (p. 8.4)

Maturity date (p. 8.4)

Principal (p. 8.4)

Face value (p. 8.4)

Coupon (p. 8.4)

Coupon rate (p. 8.4)

Convertible bond (p. 8.6)

Guaranteed bond (p. 8.6)

Serial bond (p. 8.6)

Participating bond (p. 8.6)

Floating rate bond (p. 8.6)

Callable bond (p. 8.6)

Zero-coupon bond (p. 8.6)

Sinking fund provision (p. 8.7)

Secured bond (p. 8.7)

Debenture bond (p. 8.7)

Asset-backed security (p. 8.7)

Mortgage-backed security (p. 8.7)

Yield structure (p. 8.8)

Term structure (p. 8.8)

Risk structure (p. 8.8)

Yield spread (p. 8.9)

Basis point (p. 8.9)

Yield to maturity (YTM) (p. 8.10)

Nominal rate of return (p. 8.10)

Real rate of return (p. 8.10)

Fisher effect (p. 8.10)

General obligation bond (p. 8.16)

Revenue bond (p. 8.16)

Eurobond (p. 8.16)

Foreign bond (p. 8.17)

Bond premium (p. 8.17)

Bond discount (p. 8.17)

Preferred stock (p. 8.19)

Cumulative preferred stock (p. 8.19)

Noncumulative preferred stock (p. 8.19)

Convertible preferred stock (p. 8.19)

Common stock (p. 8.20)

Fundamental analysis (p. 8.24)

Technical analysis (p. 8.25)

Efficient market hypothesis (p. 8.25)

Weak form efficiency (p. 8.26)

Semi-strong form efficiency (p. 8.26)

Strong form efficiency (p. 8.26)

Dividend growth model (p. 8.27)

Review Questions

1. Explain why it is important for a risk management professional to have an understanding of how bonds and stocks operate. (p. 8.3)

2. Describe the basic components of a bond. (pp. 8.4–8.5)

3. Describe the benefits associated with using the following types of bonds:
   a. Convertible bond (p. 8.6)

   b. Guaranteed bond (p. 8.6)

   c. Floating rate bond (p. 8.6)

   d. Zero-coupon bond (pp. 8.6–8.7)

4. Explain how a sinking fund provision for a bond affects the bond issuer. (p. 8.7)

5. Contrast a secured bond and a debenture bond. (p. 8.7)

6. Describe how the collateral backing and credit risk differ for the following bonds:
   a. Asset-backed security (p. 8.7)

   b. Mortgage-backed security (p. 8.7)

7. Identify components that either directly or indirectly affect bond pricing. (p. 8.8)

8. Describe the relationship between bond prices and interest rates. (p. 8.8)

9. Describe the two components affecting changes in bond prices when interest rates fluctuate. (p. 8.9)

10. Explain the difference between a nominal and a real rate of return and why the inflation rate is important to a typical investor. (p. 8.10)

11. Describe the relationship between nominal returns, real returns, and inflation, according to Fisher. (pp. 8.10–8.11)

12. Identify the four classifications of bonds. (p. 8.14)

13. Explain why Treasury securities have lower interest rates than corporate or agency bonds. (p. 8.14)

14. Identify reasons for which a government-sponsored enterprise (GSE) might issue federal debt. (p. 8.14)

15. Describe the operation of and security provided for the investor of the following municipal bonds:
    a. General obligation bonds (p. 8.16)

    b. Revenue bonds (p. 8.16)

16. Describe the characteristics of the following types of international bonds:
    a. Eurobonds (p. 8.17)

    b. Foreign bonds (p. 8.17)

17. Describe the importance of variations in bond valuations on balance sheets caused by financial statement preparation using SAP or GAAP accounting principles. (pp. 8.17–8.18)

18. Describe the valuation of the bond premium or discount according to statutory accounting principles (SAP). (p. 8.18)

19. Describe the bond ratings assigned by the Securities Valuation Office (SVO) of the NAIC. (p. 8.17)

20. Describe the valuation of the bond premium or discount according to generally accepted accounting principles (GAAP). (p. 8.18)

21. Contrast preferred stock dividends, common stock dividends, and bond interest payments. (pp. 8.19-8.20)

22. Identify factors that influence the price of common stock. (p. 8.22)

23. Describe the following approaches to stock pricing:
    a. Fundamental analysis (p. 8.24)

    b. Technical analysis (p. 8.25)

    c. Efficient market hypothesis (p. 8.25–8.26)

    d. Dividend growth model (pp. 8.26–8.27)

24. Describe the three forms of efficient market hypothesis.
    (p. 8.26)

25. Describe the financial presentation of stocks prepared using the following approaches:
    a. Statutory accounting principles (SAP) (p. 8.28)

    b. Generally accepted accounting principles (GAAP) (p. 8.28)

Application Questions

1. JMJ, Inc., has $1,000 face value, 7 percent coupon bonds (coupon is paid annually) on the market that have ten years until maturity. The bonds make annual coupon payments. If the yield to maturity on these bonds is 8 percent, what is the current price of the bonds?

2. C. Donavan Company, Inc., has $1,000 face value bonds on the market with nine years to maturity currently selling for $875.06. At this price, the bonds have a yield to maturity of 8 percent. What is the coupon rate of these bonds?

3. If Treasury bills are currently paying 8 percent and the inflation rate is 3 percent, what is the real rate of return on the Treasury bills?

4. ASH Corporation just paid a dividend of $1.75 per share on its common stock. The dividends are expected to grow indefinitely at a constant rate of 6 percent per year. If investors require a 12 percent return on ASH's stock, what is the price of the stock?

Answers to Assignment 8 Questions

NOTE: These answers are provided to give students a basic understanding of acceptable types of responses. They often are not the only valid answers and are not intended to provide an exhaustive response to the questions.

Review Questions

1. A risk management professional should understand how bonds and stocks operate because these assets provide insurers with the liquidity and investment income they need to operate profitably.

2. The basic components of a bond include the following:
   - Maturity date—Date on which the bond's principal is to be paid.
   - Principal (face value, or par value)—The bond's original value and the amount that will be paid at the bond's maturity date.
   - Interest rate (coupon rate)—The bond's annual interest rate stated as a percentage of its par value.
   - Rights and duties of the issuer and the buyer(s) of the bond—Corporate bondholders are creditors and do not share in the company's profits and losses. However, they must be paid before the company's shareholders receive dividends.

3. Benefits associated with using the following types of bonds include:
   a. Convertible bond—Greater chance for profit because the bond's value is supported by both its bond value and the stock conversion value.
   b. Guaranteed bond—If the guarantor is more financially stable than the issuer, having the guarantee will tend to increase the value of the bonds.
   c. Floating rate bond—Popular with issuing companies when current interest rates are high but are expected to decline because the company will not be forced to continue to pay a coupon rate that is significantly higher than the prevailing interest rate.
   d. Zero-coupon bonds—Sell at a deep discount and tend to reduce the problems related to the reinvestment of coupon payments.

4. Adding a sinking fund provision to a bond requires the bond issuer to repay a portion of the bond each year. By regularly paying off part of its debt, the issuer will have much less to pay at the bond's maturity date.

5. Secured bonds are bonds that are collateralized, or backed by specific assets of the issuer. They are secured by specific assets and have priority over the funds received in the liquidation of those assets. Debenture bonds are unsecured general obligations of the issuing corporation and have no priority over other debts in a liquidation.

6. The collateral backing and credit risk differ for these bonds, as follows:
   a. An asset-backed security is collateralized by a pool of loans, leases, or other receivables. Payments on the underlying loans or receivables are passed directly to the investors, and interest and principal are paid according to a schedule designed to appeal to the investors. Credit risk exists because the borrowers on the underlying assets could default.
   b. A mortgage-backed security is collateralized by a pool of mortgages. Credit risk differs from that of asset-backed securities because most first mortgages are guaranteed by the U.S. government through national mortgage agencies.

7. The following components either directly or indirectly affect bond pricing:
   - Current market interest rates
   - Coupon rate
   - Time to maturity
   - Yield to maturity
   - Inflation
   - Issuer's credit rating

8. The prices of bonds move inversely with changes in interest rates; when interest rates increase, the prices of bonds currently in circulation decrease.

9. Two components affecting bond price changes when interest rates fluctuate are the coupon rate and the bond's maturity. The lower the coupon rate and the longer the maturity of a bond, the more volatile its price will be.

10. The nominal rate of return is the rate of return unadjusted for the effects of inflation. The real rate of return is the rate of return adjusted for the effects of inflation. The inflation rate is important to an investor because it has a substantial effect on the purchasing power of the dollars returned on investments.

11. According to Fisher, the relationship between nominal returns, real returns, and inflation is:

    1+ Nominal rate of return = (1 + Real rate of return) × (1 + Inflation rate).

12. The four classifications of bonds are:
    (1) Federal debt
    (2) Corporate bonds
    (3) State and local debt
    (4) International bonds

13. Treasury securities have lower interest rates than corporate or agency bonds because they are guaranteed by the U.S. government for payment of principal and interest and because there is virtually no risk of default.

14. A government-sponsored enterprise (GSE) might issue federal debt to:
    - Alleviate economic recessions
    - Correct market imperfections that lead to misallocations of resources
    - Redistribute wealth
    - Channel credit into special economic sectors

15. a. General obligation bonds are secured by the full faith, credit, and taxing authority of the issuing state or municipality and are repayable from the general revenues provided by collectible taxes and from other available revenues. They offer a high level of security for the investor.

    b. Revenue bonds are payable entirely from revenue received from the users or beneficiaries of the projects financed by the bond proceeds. They involve higher risk than general obligation bonds because of the possibility that the projects financed may not bring in enough revenue to pay bondholders.

16. The following are characteristics of international bonds:
    a. Eurobonds are long-term debt instruments and are issued outside the issuer's country of origin. They typically pay interest annually, have maturities of three to seven years, and are unsecured.
    b. Foreign bonds are issued by a corporation or government outside its own country. They tend to be more highly regulated by the country in which they are issued.
17. Variations in bond valuations on balance sheets are important because they constitute a significant portion of the insurer's surplus and affect the financial ratios used by regulators, rating organizations, banks, and customers when they are analyzing the financial condition of the company.
18. According to statutory accounting principles (SAP), bond premium or discount is amortized over the life of the bond using the constant yield method of amortization, which provides for an equal rate of return for each year until the bond's maturity.
19. The value of a bond on an insurer's balance sheet depends on the rating assigned to the bond by the Securities Valuation Office (SVO). Bonds with the lowest credit risk are rated NAIC 1 and those with the highest credit risk, NAIC 6.
20. According to generally accepted accounting principles (GAAP), bonds are recorded on the balance sheet at their amortized cost if they are held-to-maturity debt securities. If a bond is not a held-to-maturity debt security, it is recorded on the balance sheet at its fair (market) value.

    Gains or losses resulting from trading securities are recorded in the current-period income statement. Gains or losses resulting from change in valuation of securities available for sale are reported as a separate amount in the statement of owners' equity.
21. Dividend payments differ as follows:
    - Preferred stock dividends—The payment of fixed dividends is not legally binding and must be voted on and approved by the board of directors. Preferred stock dividends are not tax-deductible expenses for the issuing company.
    - Common stock dividends—Not fixed dividends. If a company's earnings increase consistently, the dividend usually also increases. Common dividends are not tax deductible.
    - Bond interest—Bondholders can require payment of coupons. Not paying results in a default. Interest is tax deductible.
22. The following factors influence the price of common stock:
    - Changes in interest rates
    - Judgments concerning the firm's earning potential
    - Relative price-to-earnings ratio
    - Potential takeover and breakup value
    - Dividend payout ratio
    - Quality of management
23. The following are approaches to stock pricing:
    a. Fundamental analysis to determine the price of a stock based on an analysis of data that are fundamental to the company, such as expected growth, dividend payouts, risk, and interest rates. Compares certain variables to the Standard & Poor's averages.

b. Technical analysis involves examining market activity statistics, past prices, and market volume to detect patterns and predict a stock's price.

c. Efficient market hypothesis asserts that stock prices reflect the expectations of all market participants and that no individual investor has superior knowledge. Different forms of market efficiency lead to different stock valuation approaches.

d. The dividend growth model for valuing stocks is based on the assumption that the price of common stock is equal to the present value of the future dividend stream in perpetuity.

24. The following are three forms of efficient market hypothesis:

(1) Weak form efficiency—Asserts that current stock price reflects all historical information about the stock's price fluctuations. Assumes that successive changes in a stock's price are independent of each other, thereby rejecting technical analysis.

(2) Semi-strong form efficiency—Asserts that the current stock price reflects historical data and all current information about the stock, thereby rejecting fundamental analysis.

(3) Strong form efficiency—Asserts that stock prices reflect historical information, current public information, and insider information available only to insiders and experts. This form suggests that not even experts can consistently outperform the market.

25. The financial presentation of stocks appears as follows:

a. Statutory accounting principles (SAP)
- Preferred and common stocks are reported at the values published by the Securities Valuation Office of the NAIC.
- Preferred stocks subject to mandatory sinking funds are typically reported at amortized cost.
- Temporary market value fluctuations are reported as unrealized gains or losses in surplus.
- If a decline in market value is other than temporary, the loss is reported as a realized loss in the income statement.

b. Generally accepted accounting principles (GAAP)
- Trading securities must be recorded at fair value on the balance sheet. Gains or losses resulting from changes in valuation of trading securities are recorded in the current-period income statement.
- Securities available for sale must be reported at fair value on the balance sheet. Gains or losses resulting from changes in valuation of securities available for sale are not reported in the income statements but are reported as a separate amount in the statement of owners' equity.

Application Questions

1. The first step in determining the current price of the bond is to identify all the cash flows associated with the bond. The face value of the bond, $1,000, is payable to the bond holder in 10 years. In addition, the coupon payment paid annually for 10 years, is 7% of the face value or .07 *$1,000 = $70.00. Then the present value of the single $1,000 payment, and the present value of the series of even cash flows $70.00 for 10 years (an ordinary annuity) must be calculated.

   The present value of a single cash flow and present value of a series of even cash flows, known as the present value of an ordinary annuity can be calculated in one of three ways:

   a. Using the appropriate tables
   b. Using a financial calculator
   c. Using the formula
   a. Using the appropriate table:
      The Present Value of the face value:

Present Value of $1 at the end of n periods = $1/(1+r)^n$				
(table provided on national exam)				
PV = 1,000* PV factor(r = 8%, n = 10 years)				
No. of Periods	6%	8%	10%
10	0.5584	0.4632	0.3855

   PV = 1,000 * 0.4632
   PV = 463.20

   The Present Value of the coupon payments:

Present Value of an annuity of $1 per period for n periods = $[1-(1/(1+r)^n)]/r$	
(table provided on national exam)	
No. of Periods	8%
1	0.9259
2	1.7833
3	2.5771
4	3.3121
5	3.9927
6	4.6229
7	5.2064
8	5.7466
9	6.2469
10	6.7101

Present value of coupon payments:
   PV = 70.00* PVA factor(r = 8%, n = 10 years)
   PV = 70.00 * 6.7101
   PV = $469.71
Bond Price = PV of Face Value + PV of coupon payments
Bond Price = 463.20 + 469.71
Bond Price = $932.91

b. Using the BA II Plus Financial Calculator:
(be sure that your P/Y = 1)
Bond Payments:
FV = 1,000
PMT = 70.00
I/Y = 8
N = 10

Keystrokes:

1000	FV
70	PMT
8	I/Y
10	N
CPT	PV

Screenshot:

FV = 1,000.00
PMT = 70.00
I/Y = 8.00
N = 10
PV = 932.90

CPT – PV = -932.90 (Present value is shown as a negative number to represent how much you would have to invest today (cash outflow) to receive the 70.00 per year for the next 10 years and the $1,000 in ten years).

c. Using the formula:
Value of a Bond (Chapter 8): (Formula is provided on the national exam.)
The PV of the bond is calculated as follows:
PV = $[70.00 \times (1 \div 1.08 + 1 \div 1.08^2 + \ldots + 1 \div 1.08^{10})] + (\$1{,}000 \div 1.08^{10})$
PV^2 = (70.00 × 6.7101) + 463.20
PV = 469.71 + 463.20
PV = $932.91

2. To determine the coupon rate, the coupon payment needs to be determined. The future value ($1,000), the present value ($875.06), the interest rate (8%), and the number of time periods (9) are all given in the problem, the payment (coupon payment) needs to be determined.

The present value of a bond is equal to the present value of a single cash flow (the face value) plus the present value of an ordinary annuity (the coupon payments). The coupon payments (and therefore the coupon rate) can be calculated in one of three ways:

a. Using the appropriate tables
b. Using a financial calculator
c. Using the formula

a. Using the appropriate table:

The Present Value of the face value:

Present Value of $1 at the end of n periods = $1/(1+r)^n$			
(table provided on national exam)			
PV = 1,000* PV factor(r = 8%, n = 9 years)			
No. of Periods	6%	8%	10%
9	0.5919	0.5002	0.4241

PV = 1,000 * 0.5002
PV = 500.20

The Present Value of the coupon payments:

Present Value of an annuity of $1 per period for n periods = $[1-(1/(1+r)^n)]/r$ (table provided on national exam)	
No. of Periods	8%
1	0.9259
2	1.7833
3	2.5771
4	3.3121
5	3.9927
6	4.6229
7	5.2064
8	5.7466
9	6.2469
10	6.7101

Present value of coupon payments:
   PV = PMT* PVA factor(r = 8%, n = 9 years)
   PV = PMT * 6.2469
Bond Price = PV of Face Value + PV of coupon payments
875.06 = 500.20 + PMT*6.2469
PMT*6.2469 = 875.06 – 500.20
PMT*6.2469 = 374.86
PMT = 374.86/6.2469 = 60.01
Coupon Rate = 60.01/1,000 = 6.00%

b. Using the BA II Plus Financial Calculator:
   (be sure that your P/Y = 1)
   Bond Payments:
   Values:
   FV = 1,000
   PV = -875.06 (Present value is shown as a negative number to represent how much you would have to invest today (cash outflow) to receive the coupon payment per year for the next 9 years and the $1,000 in nine years).
   I/Y = 8
   N = 9
   PMT = ?
   The coupon rate = 60.00/1,000 = 6.00%

   Keystrokes: Screenshot:

   | 1000 | FV | | FV = | 1,000 |

   | 875.06 | +/- | PV | | PV = | -875.06 |

   | 8 | I/Y | | I/Y = | 8 |

   | 9 | N | | N = | 9 |

   | CPT | PMT | | PMT = | 60.00 |

c. Using the formula:
   Value of a Bond (Chapter 8): (Formula is provided on the national exam)
   The coupon rate of the bond is calculated as follows:
   $875.06 = [Coupon × (1 ÷ 1.08 + 1 ÷ 1.08^2 +…+ 1 ÷ 1.08^9)] + ($1,000 ÷ 1.08^9)
   $875.06 = (Coupon × 6.246888) + $500.25.
   Therefore:
   Coupon × 6.246888 = $875.06-500.25
   Coupon × 6.246888 = $374.81
   Coupon = $374.81/6.246888
   Coupon = $60.00
   Coupon rate = 6.00% of the $1,000 face value of the bond.

3. The real rate of return on the Treasury bills is calculated using the Fisher Effect formula (provided on the national exam) as follows:

    Fisher Effect (Chapter 8):

    (1 + Nominal rate) = (1 + Real rate) × (1 + Inflation rate)

    (1 + 0.08) = (1 + Real rate) × (1 + 0.03)

    (1 + Real rate) = 1.08 ÷ 1.03

    (1 + Real rate) = 1.0485

    Real rate = 0.0485, or 4.85%.

4. The current price of the stock is calculated using the dividend growth model (provided on the national exam), as follows:

    Dividend Growth Model (Chapter 8): $V_0 = D_1 / (r-g)$

    Price = Dividend at next dividend date ÷ (Market return − Annual dividend growth rate)

    Price = (1.06 × $1.75) ÷ (12% − 6%)

        = $1.855 ÷ 6%

        = $30.92.

Direct Your Learning

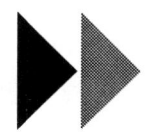

ASSIGNMENT 9

Operating Environment and Corporate Finance

Educational Objectives

After learning the content of this assignment, you should be able to:

1. Explain how an insurer's legal and regulatory environment can affect its operations.

2. Explain how an insurer's economic environment, both financial and nonfinancial, can affect its business.

3. Explain why it is difficult to develop a concise theory for the cause of insurance cycles.

4. Describe the business strategies normally used by insurers during the different phases of an underwriting cycle.

5. Explain how the following factors influence underwriting cycles:
   - Investment income
   - Capacity
   - Return on equity

6. Explain the effect of supply and demand on insurance underwriting cycles.

7. Contrast the effects of underwriting cycles on insurers and agents and brokers.

8. Compare the structure of insurance industry profit cycles to that of the cycles in other industries.

9. Explain why the study of underwriting cycles is important.

Study Materials

Required Reading:
- Finance for Risk Management and Insurance Professionals
  - Chapter 9

Study Aids:
- SMART Online Practice Exams
- SMART Study Aids
  - Review Notes and Flash Cards—Assignment 9

Outline

- **Legal and Regulatory Environment**
- **Economic Environment**
- **Insurance Industry Cycles**
  - A. Understanding Insurance Industry Cycles
  - B. Underwriting Cycles
  - C. Phases of the Underwriting Cycle
  - D. Factors Influencing the Underwriting Cycle
    1. Investment Income
    2. Capacity
    3. Return on Equity
  - E. Cycles and Pricing—Supply and Demand
    1. Supply
    2. Demand
  - F. Effects of the Underwriting Cycle
    1. Insurers
    2. Agents and Brokers
  - G. Profit Cycles in Other Industries
- **Study of Underwriting Cycles**
- **Summary**

study tips: Try to establish a study area away from any distractions, to be used only for studying.

Key Words and Phrases

Define or describe each of the words and phrases listed below.

Reputational risk (p. 9.4)

Socioeconomics (p. 9.6)

Structural change (p. 9.7)

Business cycle (p. 9.7)

Profit cycle (p. 9.7)

Underwriting cycle (p. 9.7)

Hard market (p. 9.9)

Soft market (p. 9.9)

Reunderwriting (p. 9.10)

Cash-flow underwriting (p. 9.12)

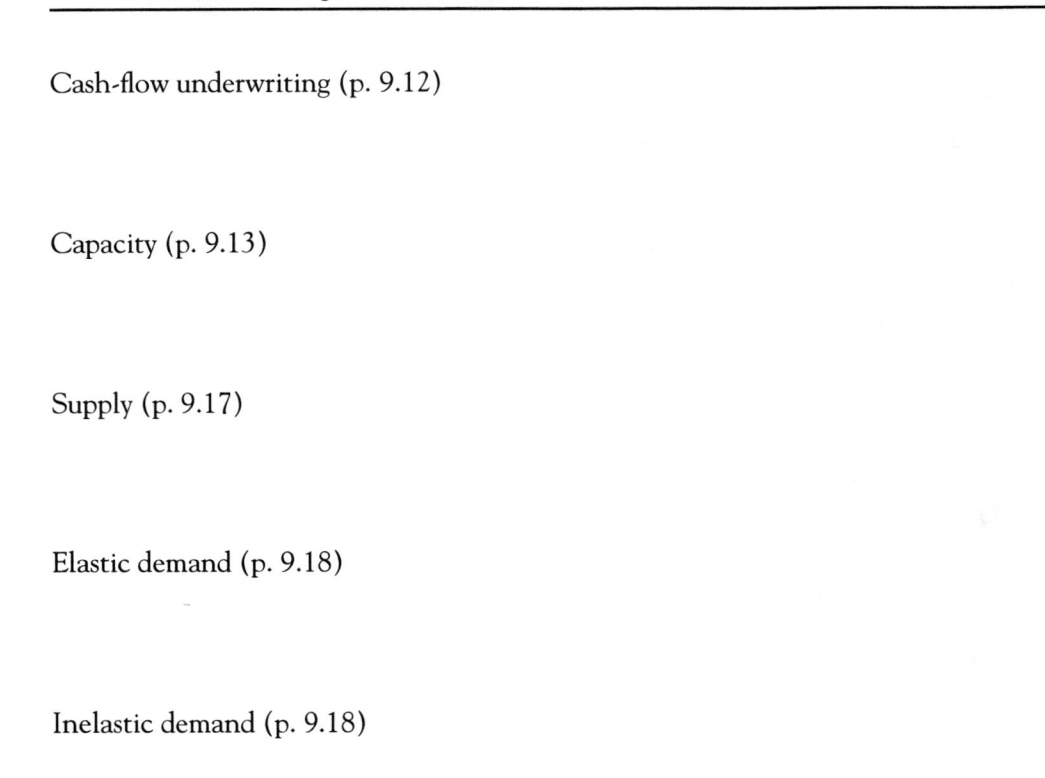

Capacity (p. 9.13)

Supply (p. 9.17)

Elastic demand (p. 9.18)

Inelastic demand (p. 9.18)

Review Questions

1. List the components of an insurer's legal and regulatory environment. (p. 9.3)

2. Explain how an insurer's operation might be affected by the legal and regulatory environment. (p. 9.4)

3. Identify possible sources of reputational risk for an insurer. (p. 9.5)

4. Explain how cultural and demographic information might affect the economic environment of an insurer. (p. 9.5)

5. Identify population characteristics that are part of the demographic environment. (p. 9.5)

6. List socioeconomic factors that could affect the insurance industry. (p. 9.6)

7. Explain why it is difficult to construct a theory to explain insurance cycles. (p. 9.7)

8. Identify what structural change within the insurance industry involves. (p. 9.7)

9. List three phases of the business cycle. (p. 9.7)

10. Explain how the terms "profit cycle" and "underwriting cycle" differ. (pp. 9.7–9.8)

11. Describe actions that insurers typically take to maintain surplus when experiencing the following underwriting cycles:
    a. Underwriting profits (p. 9.8)

    b. Underwriting losses (p. 9.8)

12. Explain how underwriting profitability defines the hard and soft markets in the insurance industry. (p. 9.9)

13. Describe potential insurer strategies to achieve the following results in response to the underwriting cycle:
    a. Price reduction in a soft market (p. 9.9)

    b. Increased profitability in a hard market (p. 9.10)

14. Describe how increased capital from new competitors in a hard market affects the underwriting cycle. (p. 9.10)

15. Explain why regulators are concerned when extreme hard market or soft market patterns occur in the underwriting cycle. (p. 9.11)

16. Identify the factors influencing the underwriting cycle. (p. 9.12)

17. Describe why underwriting managers generally dislike using cash-flow underwriting. (p. 9.12)

18. Identify the traditional measure of insurer capacity. (p. 9.13)

19. Explain what is meant by the point of price equilibrium. (p. 9.16)

20. Describe how decreasing prices and increasing supply affect the point of price equilibrium. (p. 9.16)

21. Describe the factors affecting the supply of property-casualty insurance. (pp. 9.17–9.18)

22. Describe how premium price variations might affect the following:
    a. Consumer demand for insurance (p. 9.18)

    b. Insurer premium rates (p. 9.19)

23. Describe how insurers typically respond to the soft and hard markets of the underwriting cycle. (p. 9.19)

24. Describe how agents and brokers adapt to the underwriting cycle. (p. 9.20)

25. Explain how considering profit cycles in other industries might help an insurance professional when underwriting or settling claims. (p. 9.20)

26. Describe a problem that might occur if the insurance underwriting cycle is in a hard market and the insured's profit cycle is in an expansion phase. (p. 9.20)

27. Identify two insights regarding underwriting cycles that are provided by studying historical trends. (p. 9.21)

Application Questions

1. An insured has been accused of accounting irregularities in its financial reporting; however, it has not been proved that these irregularities actually occurred. Why could this accusation alone have a negative effect on the insured's business?

2. Name two socioeconomic factors that could affect the insurance industry, and explain the possible effects.

3. Historically, insurance industry underwriting cycles have consisted of a period of underwriting profits followed by a period of underwriting losses, as measured by the industry's combined ratio. Explain how the results of the study of past underwriting cycle factors have been used to predict the length and severity of future underwriting cycles.

4. Insurance underwriting cycles are affected by a number of factors. One of the factors that precipitate changes in an underwriting cycle is pricing. Explain how supply and demand affect the price of insurance and therefore affect underwriting cycles.

5. LMO, Inc., is a manufacturer that is currently in the expansion stage of its operating cycle. LMO's insurer is in the hard market phase of its underwriting cycle. Explain how the differing operating cycle phases affect the insurance market relationship between LMO and its insurer.

6. As the insurance markets have become more competitive, insurers have become fully subject to the laws of supply and demand, making underwriting cycles more difficult to predict. Explain how the study of underwriting cycles helps an insurer in developing business strategies.

Answers to Assignment 9 Questions

NOTE: These answers are provided to give students a basic understanding of acceptable types of responses. They often are not the only valid answers and are not intended to provide an exhaustive response to the questions.

Review Questions

1. Components of an insurer's legal and regulatory environment include the laws, rules, regulations, prescribed practices, and ethical standards that apply in all of the jurisdictions in which the company operates.

2. From an operational standpoint, the legal and regulatory environment can limit or enhance an insurer in the following areas:
   - Ability to implement business plans
   - Ability to make strategic and operational decisions
   - Ability to allocate resources
   - Ability to adapt to changes in the business environment that will affect its competitive position and financial condition
   - Ability to resolve policy interpretation disputes outside of court

3. Sources of possible reputational risk for an insurer include the following:
   - Negative publicity from court cases or regulatory issues
   - Consumer issues
   - Safety issues
   - Environmental issues

4. The cultural environment, which includes the patterns and norms that regulate society's behavior, can affect the types and amounts of insurance that individuals are willing to purchase. Demographic information, including population characteristics, can greatly affect the insurance markets and can be used in the establishment of market segmentations and development of new insurance products.

5. The demographic environment includes factors such as age distributions, births, deaths, marital status, gender, education, wealth, and geographic location.

6. The following socioeconomic factors could affect the insurance industry:
   - New technologies
   - Changes in the physical environment
   - Ecological changes
   - Increased use of litigation and variability in the dollar amount of judgments among jurisdictions

7. It is difficult to construct a theory to explain insurance cycles because the operating environment of insurers is influenced by many outside factors and because insurers must continually adapt to the pressures from within the insurance business, such as competition and regulation.

8. Structural change within the insurance industry involves:
   - New products and services
   - New providers taking on new roles
   - Changes in government attitude toward business practices
   - Changes in government regulation

9. The three phases of the business cycle are:
   (1) Recession
   (2) Recovery
   (3) Expansion

10. The underwriting cycle is the recurring increase and decrease in underwriting profits and premiums. The profit cycle is based on the sum of underwriting income and investment income, as opposed to underwriting performance alone.

11. Insurers maintain surplus in the following economic environments:
    a. When experiencing underwriting profits, an insurer may reduce premium rates and offer broader coverage to increase its market share.
    b. When experiencing underwriting losses, an insurer may need to increase premium rates and restrict the availability of coverage to increase underwriting profits.

12. In a hard market, insurer competition diminishes, buyers have difficulty finding coverage, premiums increase, and insurer profitability rises. When insurers believe they have enough surplus to reduce premiums and write additional insurance to increase market share, the soft market begins and competition becomes intense as insurers start to reduce premiums and expand coverages. Insurers eventually experience decreased profitability, which leads again to the beginning of a hard market cycle.

13. Potential insurer strategies to achieve results in response to the underwriting cycle include the following:
    a. Price reduction in a soft market—Reducing rates, increasing the use of rate credits, broadening the terms of coverage, and loosening underwriting standards
    b. Increased profitability in a hard market—Raising rates; reunderwriting; and, as necessary, imposing surcharges, deductibles, or nonrenewals

14. Increased capital is often needed to satisfy insurance regulatory restrictions on insurers' written premiums relative to their policyholders' surplus. Increased capital obtained from new competitors in a hard market satisfies demand, fuels competition, and causes the underwriting cycle to turn.

15. Regulators are concerned when extreme patterns occur in the underwriting cycle. In a hard market, they must address insurance coverage availability and affordability problems. A prolonged soft market can lead to insurer insolvencies.

16. The following factors influence the underwriting cycle:
    - Investment income
    - Capacity
    - Return on equity

17. Underwriting managers generally dislike using cash-flow underwriting because it undermines underwriting discipline and because investment income can mask poor underwriting decisions.

18. The traditional measure of insurer capacity is the ratio of premiums written to policyholders' surplus.

19. The point of price equilibrium is the point at which buyers and sellers are both satisfied with the product's price.

20. Pricing related to the supply of and demand for insurance affects the point of price equilibrium. When underlying demand decreases and supply increases, the point of price equilibrium decreases.

21. The following factors affect the supply of property-casualty insurance:
    - Reinsurance—Expands an insurer's capacity by allowing it to increase gross premium writings.
    - Difficulty of exit—Increases the insurance supply because once capital is committed to the insurance industry, it tends to stay committed due to regulatory requirements.
    - Dedicated capital—Increases the insurance supply because an insurer licensed only to write insurance has to dedicate its capital to compete for available business.
    - Underreserving—Artificially inflates surplus and thereby increases capacity. Although it can initially increase supply, ultimately the underreserving must be corrected, resulting in a decrease in supply.
    - Profit expectations—Uncertain and shifting, possibly resulting in the use of risk management techniques and alternative risk transfer products.

22. Price variations might have the following effect:
    a. Consumer demand for insurance—When premiums decrease, insureds might purchase higher limits, add coverages, or purchase additional policies. Increasing premiums may cause insureds to reduce coverages, eliminate coverage, or use alternative methods of risk financing.
    b. Insurer premium rates—Price will not generally influence demand significantly because it is not necessary to purchase two or more policies covering the same property. Also, the decision to purchase insurance required by statute is not affected by price.

23. In soft markets, premium pricing generally decreases and insurers develop specialized products and cultivate niche markets. As the market hardens, they become more selective about the accounts they are willing to accept and may limit the number of producers who represent them to those with the best accounts.

24. In a soft market, competition for accounts with other producers is intense. Price reductions occur, and producer commission income is reduced. The potential for insurer insolvencies increases, exposing agents and brokers to professional liability. In hard markets, producers actively market accounts to insurers. Insurance prices increase along with commission income.

25. This information is useful to insurance professionals because profit cycles in these industries can provide insight into an insured's current financial condition and its future prospects.

26. If the insurance underwriting cycle is in a hard market and the insured's profit cycle is in an expansion phase, a disruption in the insurance market for that industry could occur due to tightening of insurance availability.

27. The following two insights are provided by studying historical underwriting cycles:
    (1) The nature of underwriting cycles has changed as insurance markets have evolved; as insurance markets became more competitive, insurers became subject to the laws of supply and demand.
    (2) Certain fundamentals of underwriting cycles have remained the same; insurance buyers tend to deal with crises of availability by creating risk financing alternatives.

Application Questions

1. Even though the company has not been found guilty of intentionally creating these accounting irregularities, the company has a significant exposure to reputational risk. Reputational risk deals with the perceptions of a company that are held by its customers, suppliers, lenders, regulators, and shareholders. If these stakeholders have a negative perception of the company, it could cause a significant loss of market value. For example, existing customers may leave and new customers may not be added. This loss of business, along with the negative perception of possible accounting irregularities, could negatively affect the value of the company's stock and possibly its credit rating. A downgrade in a credit rating could result in lenders' no longer being willing to provide additional loans, thereby creating liquidity problems.

2. Two socioeconomic factors that could affect the insurance industry are increased crowding on roads and new safety features in automobiles. While the increased crowding on roads is likely to lead to an increased number of auto claims each year, the new safety features in automobiles made possible by new technologies may reduce the amount of the claims. These aspects of an insurer's operating environment must be considered when developing coverages, deductibles, policy limits, and premium rates.

3. Although most of the factors affecting the underwriting cycle have been identified by examining past cycles, changes in the insurance marketplace in response to each of these factors during past underwriting cycles has reduced their predictive value, thereby increasing the difficulty of determining when the next phase of the underwriting cycle will begin.

4. In insurance, supply is the aggregate willingness of all insurers to assume risk at a given time. At any point in the underwriting cycle, a change in the supply of insurance can have an effect. An increase in supply can have a softening effect on the market, and a decrease in supply can have a hardening effect. Supply differs from capacity in that capacity reflects the total amount of risk insurers can write relative to their surplus, regardless of their willingness to do so.

   In insurance, demand is the willingness to buy insurance. Insurance demand has attributes of elasticity, a willingness to purchase that varies significantly with price, and inelasticity, a willingness to purchase that does not vary with price. When premiums decrease, insureds may increase coverage or purchase additional policies. If premiums increase, insureds may reduce coverages or use alternative methods of risk financing. However, changes in premium rates do not generally result in significant changes in the amount of insurance demanded. This is because it is not necessary to purchase two policies covering the same property regardless of premium. Also, prices do not change the demand for insurance that is required by statute. Overall, insurance prices are driven more by the supply of insurance than by the demand for it.

5. Because LMO, Inc., is in the expansion phase of its operating cycle, it is looking to purchase additional amounts of insurance. It is also likely that LMO requires its capital to finance its growth. Therefore, it will be important to LMO to keep its insurance premiums as low as possible. LMO's insurer is in the hard market stage of its underwriting cycle, which means it is probably limiting its supply of insurance by being extremely tight with its underwriting guidelines, increasing premiums, and limiting the use of premium payment plans. Because LMO and its insurer are in different phases of their profit and underwriting cycles, there is a significant disruption in their dealings in the insurance market.

6. The study of underwriting cycles has shown that certain related fundamentals have remained constant. One constant is the tendency of insurance buyers to deal with crises of availability and perceptions of excessive or unaffordable prices by creating risk financing alternatives. Although this tendency has created structural changes in the insurance industry, it also means that the crises are relatively short lived and that the cycles persist. Studying underwriting cycles also helps in developing business strategy. Understanding the competitiveness of the insurance markets—many buyers and sellers, similar products, and low barriers to entry—allows insurers to develop competitive strategies. These strategies are likely to involve plans to reduce market competition by being the only seller, selling a different product, or raising barriers to entry.

Direct Your Learning

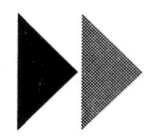

Insurer Investment Strategies

Educational Objectives

After learning the content of this assignment, you should be able to:

1. Given appropriate data, calculate the annual rates of return for given securities.
2. Explain how the most commonly used market indexes are structured for use in reviewing historical market results.
3. Explain how the historical market return performance of stocks and bonds can be used in setting expected returns.
4. Describe common types of investment-related financial risks that affect securities.
5. Explain the following quantitative measures of risk:
   - Variance
   - Standard deviation
   - Coefficient of variation
   - Value at risk
   - Beta
6. Explain how the following affect investment portfolio management:
   - Modern portfolio theory
   - Risk-return trade-off
   - Investment diversification
   - Beta and risk premium
   - Equity portfolio risk
   - Capital asset pricing model and the security market line
   - Investment strategy
7. Describe the following issues involved in managing an insurer's bond portfolios:
   - Cash matching and interest rate risk
   - Matching investment and liability duration

Study Materials

Required Reading:
- Finance for Risk Management and Insurance Professionals
  - Chapter 10

Study Aids:
- SMART Online Practice Exams
- SMART Study Aids
  - Review Notes and Flash Cards—Assignment 10

Outline

- **Historical Market Returns**
    - A. Annual Rates of Return
    - B. Market Indexes
    - C. Expected Returns
- **Common Investment-Related Risks**
    - A. Market Risk
    - B. Credit Risk
    - C. Interest Rate Risk
    - D. Liquidity Risk
- **Quantitative Measures of Risk**
    - A. Variance
    - B. Standard Deviation
    - C. Coefficient of Variation
    - D. Value at Risk
    - E. Beta
- **Investment Portfolio Management**
    - A. Modern Portfolio Theory
    - B. The Risk-Return Trade-Off
    - C. Investment Diversification
    - D. Beta and the Risk Premium
    - E. Equity Portfolio Risk
    - F. The Capital Asset Pricing Model and the Security Market Line
        1. Risk-Free Returns
        2. Market Risk Premiums
        3. Market Risk Assumed
    - G. Investment Strategy
    - H. Bond Portfolios
        1. Cash Matching and Interest Rate Risk
        2. Matching Investment and Liability Duration
- **Summary**

study tips — Writing notes as you read your materials will help you remember key pieces of information.

Key Words and Phrases
Define or describe each of the words and phrases listed below.

Dividend yield (p. 10.5)

Percentage gain (p. 10.5)

Percentage total return (p. 10.5)

Market index (p. 10.7)

Market risk, or systematic risk (p. 10.11)

Company-specific risk, or unsystematic risk (p. 10.11)

Credit risk (p. 10.12)

Liquidity risk (p. 10.12)

Variance (p. 10.13)

Standard deviation (p. 10.14)

Coefficient of variation (p. 10.15)

Value at risk (p. 10.16)

Portfolio optimization (p. 10.17)

Risk-return trade-off (p. 10.17)

Diversification (p. 10.18)

Correlation coefficient (p. 10.19)

Beta (p. 10.20)

Risk premium (p. 10.21)

Efficient frontier (p. 10.21)

Capital asset pricing model (CAPM) (p. 10.22)

Security market line (SML) (p. 10.22)

Cash matching (p. 10.27)

Reinvestment risk (p. 10.27)

Duration (p. 10.28)

Portfolio immunization (p. 10.29)

Review Questions

1. Identify the factors an insurer uses in developing investment portfolio strategies. (p. 10.4)

2. Describe two ways in which an investor can earn an annual return on an investment in stocks or bonds. (p. 10.5)

3. Describe the following measures of return for stocks and how each is calculated:
   a. Dividend yield (pp. 10.5, 10.7)

   b. Percentage gain (pp. 10.5, 10.7)

   c. Percentage total return (pp. 10.5, 10.7)

4. Explain why the effect of inflation should be considered when evaluating the return on investment. (p. 10.7)

5. Describe how an investor might use a market index. (pp. 10.7–10.8)

6. Identify the indexes commonly used for bonds. (p. 10.8)

7. Describe the following stock market indexes:
   a. Dow Jones Industrial Average (DJIA) (pp. 10.8–10.9)

   b. S&P 500 Index (p. 10.9)

   c. Nasdaq Composite Index (p. 10.9)

   d. Russell 2000 Index (p. 10.9)

   e. Morgan Stanley Capital International, Inc.'s MSCI EAFE Index (p. 10.9)

8. Describe how the following measures of past rates of return can be used to set expected returns:
   a. Arithmetic average of past returns (p. 10.10)

   b. Geometric average total rate of return (pp. 10.10–10.11)

9. Describe the circumstances in which the geometric average return of a product would be the appropriate method of calculating expected return. (p. 10.11)

10. Explain why it is important to use indicators in addition to historical market returns to assess the effect of certain risks on an investment security. (p. 10.11)

11. Describe the common investment-related risks. (pp. 10.11–10.12)

12. Explain the effectiveness of diversification regarding market risk and company-specific risk. (p. 10.11)

13. Describe how the following risk metrics are used to measure the likelihood of not achieving the expected average rate of return on an investment:

    a. Variance (p. 10.13)

    b. Standard deviation (p. 10.14)

    c. Coefficient of variation (p. 10.15)

    d. Value at risk (p. 10.16)

    e. Beta (p. 10.16)

14. Identify one drawback of using the standard deviation as a measure of risk. (p. 10.15)

15. Identify situations in which the coefficient of variation is not useful as a measure of risk. (p. 10.15)

16. Describe methods that may be used to estimate the value at risk for any given small probability of loss. (p. 10.16)

17. Identify the considerations included in a comprehensive investment portfolio management program. (p. 10.17)

18. Describe the four steps in the decision process associated with the modern portfolio theory. (p. 10.17)

19. Identify the economic and financial theory assumption concerning risk that is made about investors and managers who are choosing investments. (p. 10.18)

20. Describe the significance of a correlation coefficient between two variables of +1, –1, and zero. (p. 10.19)

21. Identify the advantages of using the beta as a measure of risk when assessing the volatility of a stock. (p. 10.21)

22. Describe the indications of beta values regarding stock volatility. (p. 10.21)

23. Explain why a company strives to develop the efficient frontier regarding investment portfolios. (pp. 10.21–10.22)

24. Describe the three elements used in the capital asset pricing model (CAPM). (pp. 10.22–10.25)

25. Explain why integrating investment strategy with other functional areas of the company is important for insurers. (p. 10.25)

26. Identify the most important objective of bond portfolio management. (p. 10.26)

27. Identify additional sources of risk to which an investor is exposed when investing in bonds. (p. 10.26)

28. List two important characteristics of bond duration. (p. 10.28)

Application Questions

1. Complete the following table for each share of the securities listed.

Security	Value at beginning of year	Value at end of year	Annual dividend received	Dividend yield	Percentage gain	Percentage total return
A	$25.00	$26.50	$0.75	?	?	?
B	?	$35.00	$1.75	5%	?	?
C	$10.00	12.00	?	?	?	23%
D	$15.00	?	$0.45	?	15%	?

2. When portfolio managers diversify their portfolios, the expected rate of return on the portfolio will be equal to the weighted average of the expected return of each security held. Explain why the standard deviation of the portfolio either is or is not the weighted average of the standard deviation of each security held.

3. A portfolio manager must consider the amount of return a security should earn to fully compensate the owner of the security for risks taken by owning the stock. Explain how the capital asset pricing model can be used to identify the price of a security.

4. A portfolio manager is considering two alternative $100,000 investments. The annual return for the two investments is listed in the following table, along with several metrics derived from these annual returns. Using the information in the table, choose the preferred investment and explain the reasons for your choice.

Year	Annual Return Inv. A	Annual Return Inv. B
Current year	10.8%	10.2%
Current year −1	−1.0%	14.3%
Current year −2	22.3%	13.6%
Current year −3	13.1%	13.2%
Current year −4	18.0%	12.4%
Current year −5	−2.0%	11.8%
Current year −6	15.0%	11.1%
Current year −7	10.0%	10.3%
Current year −8	15.0%	10.6%
Current year −9	20.0%	10.9%
Arithmetic Average	12.1%	11.9%
Geometric Average	11.8%	11.8%
Variance	0.007	0.0002
Standard Deviation	0.081	0.015
Coefficient of Variation	0.687	0.123

Answers to Assignment 10 Questions

NOTE: These answers are provided to give students a basic understanding of acceptable types of responses. They often are not the only valid answers and are not intended to provide an exhaustive response to the questions.

Review Questions

1. An insurer uses the following factors in developing investment portfolio strategies:
   - Historical information—Gives investors an idea of the risks and returns that certain investments might generate
   - Financial and risk metrics—Measure the likelihood of not achieving the expected average rate of return, including variance, standard deviation, coefficient of variation, value at risk, and beta
   - Various investment and portfolio theories—Considers modern portfolio theory, risk-return trade-off, investment diversification, beta and risk premium, equity portfolio risk, capital asset pricing model, investment strategy, and matching investment and liability duration of bond and underwriting portfolios

2. The annual return an investor can earn on an investment in stocks or bonds comes from two sources: (1) periodic payments in the form of stock dividends or bond interest and (2) a gain or loss based on the change in the value of the investment from the beginning of the year to the end of the year.

3. The following are measures of return for stocks:
   a. Dividend yield—The amount of dividends received per share of stock owned, expressed as a percentage of the value of the investment at the beginning of the period. Calculated as follows:

   Dividend ÷ Share price.

   b. Percentage gain—The capital gain or loss based on the change in the value of the investment from the beginning of the period. Calculated as follows:

   Capital gain ÷ Share price at the beginning of the year.

   c. Percentage total return—The total of the dividend received and the capital gain for the period, expressed as a percentage of the value of the investment at the beginning of the period. Calculated as follows:

   (Capital gain + Dividend) ÷ Share price at the beginning of the year.

4. The effect of inflation should be considered when evaluating the return on investment to determine the purchasing power of the return.

5. An investor might use a market index for the following reasons:
   - To measure the return on the particular market or sector represented by the index
   - To serve as a benchmark against which portfolio, financial, or economic performance is measured
   - To reflect the returns for a given market or industry

6. The following indexes are commonly used for bonds:
   - Lehman Brothers Aggregate Bond Index—Consists of price appreciation or depreciation plus income, expressed as a percentage of the original investment

- Ten-year U.S. Treasury bond—Backed by the United States government; often considered the standard for long-term bond investments

7. The following are widely used stock market indexes:
   a. Dow Jones Industrial Average (Dow, or DJIA)—Consists of the stocks of thirty large U.S. companies
   b. S&P 500 Index—A market-weighted index that tracks 500 companies in leading industries
   c. Nasdaq Composite Index—Measures all common stocks, domestic and international, listed on the National Association of Securities Dealers Automated Quotation System (Nasdaq) stock market
   d. Russell 2000 Index—Measures the overall performance of the small to mid-size market capitalization stocks
   e. Morgan Stanley Capital International, Inc.'s MSCI EAFE Index—Free-float-adjusted market capitalization index designed to measure developed market equity performance, excluding that of the U.S. and Canada

8. The following measures of past rates of return can be used to set expected returns, as shown below:
   a. The arithmetic average of past returns is calculated as follows:

   $$\text{Sum of annual returns} \div \text{Number of years}.$$

   b. The geometric average total rate of return measures the compound annual average rate at which the asset's value has grown during the period under observation. It is calculated as follows:

   $$[(1 + \text{Return } 1) \times (1 + \text{Return } 2) \times \ldots \times (1 + \text{Return } n)]^{(1 \div n)} - 1.0$$

9. The geometric average return of a product would be the appropriate method of calculating expected return if several differing rates of return (such as interest rates) contribute to a product's return.

10. It is important to use indicators in addition to historical market returns to assess the effect of certain risks on an investment security because historical market returns do not show the types of risks that are involved. Investors need to understand which risks commonly affect the securities in which they are considering investing and how those risks can affect returns.

11. The following are common investment-related risks:
    - Risks that are common to the overall market or a specific market segment. These risks are called market risks, or systematic risks.
    - Risk that a debtor will not repay the amount owed, which is called credit risk.
    - Uncertainty about the future value of an investment because of changes in the general level of interest rates, which is called interest rate risk.
    - The risk that an asset cannot be sold on short notice without incurring a loss, which is called liquidity risk.

12. Diversification is not an effective way to eliminate market risk because the prices of individual securities tend to follow broad market swings, independent of an individual company's performance. Company-specific risk affects a specific company or small group of companies, so diversification is an effective way to eliminate this type of risk.

13. The following risk metrics are used to measure the likelihood of not achieving the expected average rate of return on an investment:
    a. Variance—Used to quantify investment risk by measuring the deviation of the values of an investment from the average of the investment's values during a specific period. The larger the variance, the more often the actual returns will differ from the average returns and the wider those differences may be. The variance is calculated by dividing the sum of the squared deviations by the number of elements included in the data set less one:

    $$\text{Sum of squared deviations} \div (n-1).$$

    b. Standard deviation—Measure of the variability between each value in a data set and the data set's mean. The larger the standard deviation, the more volatile the returns of the stock. The standard deviation is the square root of the variance:

    $$\sqrt{\text{Variance}}$$

    c. Coefficient of variation—Facilitates the comparison of two data sets with substantially different means. The variation of actual values can be compared with the variation of expected values. The coefficient of variation is calculated by dividing the standard deviation by the mean or expected value:

    $$\text{Standard deviation} \div \text{Mean or expected value}$$

    d. Value at risk—Measure of potential dollar losses from an unlikely adverse event affecting an investment portfolio in an otherwise normal market environment. It is expressed as a dollar amount.
    e. Beta—Measures the movement of an individual stock's return in relation to the market.

14. One drawback of the standard deviation as a measure of risk is that the larger the actual values in a data set, the larger its standard deviation will typically be. Comparing the standard deviation of two or more data sets in which elements are of different magnitude can be misleading.

15. The coefficient of variation is not useful as a measure of risk when the mean approaches zero or is zero.

16. The following methods may be used to estimate the value at risk for any given small probability of loss:
    - Parametric statistical methods—Mathematical procedures that assume that the occurrence of the variables being assessed belongs to a known probability distribution
    - Simulation techniques—Models that create an artificial environment designed to mirror the actual environment

17. The following considerations are included in a comprehensive investment portfolio management program:
    - Modern portfolio theory
    - Risk-return trade-off
    - Investment diversification
    - Beta and risk premium
    - Equity portfolio risk
    - Capital asset pricing model
    - Investment strategy
    - Matching investment and liability duration

18. The following four steps are part of the decision process associated with the modern portfolio theory:
    (1) Security valuation—Assess securities in terms of expected return and expected risk to compare the relative attractiveness of the investments
    (2) Asset allocation—Determine the proportion of assets to be allocated to each security category
    (3) Portfolio optimization—Arrange a stock portfolio so that risks are minimized and rates of return are maximized
    (4) Performance measurement—Monitor the earnings, dividends, and price of the stock over time

19. The economic and financial theory assumption concerning risk is that investors and managers are risk averse and will generally choose investments with the least risk.

20. Correlation coefficients have the following significance between two variables:
    - Correlation coefficient of +1: Perfectly positively correlated, and price changes always move in the same direction
    - Correlation coefficient of −1: Perfectly negatively correlated, and price changes always move in the opposite direction
    - Correlation coefficient of zero: Uncorrelated, and price movements are totally unrelated

21. Advantages of using the beta as a measure of risk when assessing stock volatility include:
    - Interpreting its value is reasonably straightforward.
    - The beta can also be used as an indication of the volatility of an entire portfolio.

22. Beta values indicate the following:
    - Beta of 1: The stock has the same risk as the market as a whole; indicates average risk.
    - Beta greater than 1: The stock has greater price volatility than the overall market and can be considered riskier.
    - Beta less than 1: The stock has less price volatility than the overall market and could be considered less risky.

23. A company strives to develop the efficient frontier regarding investment portfolios so the portfolio combinations best meet its needs. Typically, investors combine securities to generate the highest expected return for a given level of risk or choose securities that have the lowest risk for a given expected return.

24. The following three elements are used in the capital asset pricing model (CAPM):
    (1) Risk-free returns—The return on a risk-free investment establishes a baseline against which the returns of all other securities can be compared.
    (2) Market risk premiums—The difference between the expected return on the market portfolio (r_m) and the risk-free rate of return (r_f).
    (3) Market risk assumed—Reflected by the beta of the individual stock or the entire portfolio.

25. Integrating investment strategy with other functional areas of the company is important for insurers because invested assets are a primary source of funds available to pay losses. The investment strategy and portfolio management must recognize the relationship between the investment portfolio and the company's underwriting decisions.

26. The most important objective of bond portfolio management is to structure the portfolio so that the amount and timing of investment cash flows correspond to the firm's expected cash outflows.

27. An investor is exposed to the following additional sources of risk when investing in bonds:
   - Credit risk—Uncertainty about an issuer's ability to make the required principal and interest payments as they come due
   - Interest rate risk—Uncertainty about an asset's value associated with changes in market-determined interest rates
28. Two important characteristics of bond duration are:
   (1) The duration of a zero-coupon bond is always equal to its time to maturity.
   (2) The duration of a bond that pays interest over its life will always be less than its time to maturity.

Application Questions

1. Complete the following table for each share of the securities listed.

Security	Value at beginning of year	Value at end of year	Annual dividend received	Dividend yield	Percentage gain	Percentage total return
A	$25.00	$26.50	$0.75	3%	6%	9%
B	**$35.00**	$35.00	$1.75	5%	0	5%
C	$10.00	$12.00	**$0.30**	3%	20%	23%
D	$15.00	**$17.25**	$0.45	3%	15%	18%

Calculated as follows:

Security	Value at beginning of year	Value at end of year	Annual dividend received	Dividend yield	Percentage gain	Percentage total return
A	$25.00	$26.50	$0.75	$0.75 ÷ $25.00 [1]	($26.50 − $25.00) ÷ $25.00 [2]	DY + PG [3]
B*	$1.75 ÷ 0.05 [1]	$35.00	$1.75	5%	(Value EY − Value BY) ÷ Value BY [2]	DY + PG [3]
C*	$10.00	$12.00	$10 × DY [3]	PTR − PG [2]	($12 − $10) ÷ $10 [1]	23%
D	$15.00	Value BY × (1 + PG) [2]	$0.45	3% [1]	15%	DY + PG [3]

* Calculate the variables in the order indicated in the upper right corner.

2. The standard deviation of the portfolio is less than the weighted average of the standard deviations of the individual securities in the portfolio. This is because the returns of all securities do not move in unison. The measure of the degree to which the securities do move in unison is their correlation coefficient, which ranges from +1 to –1. Securities whose prices always move in unison have a correlation coefficient of +1 and are considered perfectly positively correlated. If their prices always move in opposite directions, their correlation coefficient is –1 and they are considered perfectly negatively correlated. If the price movements of each security are totally unrelated, the correlation coefficient is zero and they are considered uncorrelated. It is not necessary to have negatively correlated stock to lower the risk of the portfolio; the only requirement for reducing the risk of the portfolio through diversification is that the stocks are not perfectly positively correlated.

3. The capital asset pricing model uses three components to determine the expected price of a security: a risk-free return, an expected overall market return, and the security's beta. The risk-free return is the return that can be earned by investing in a total risk-free security. The risk-free rate is normally represented by the amount that can be earned by investing in long-term U.S. Treasury securities. The market return is the expected market rate of return for all the securities in the market. The difference between the market return and the risk-free return is the market risk premium for the overall market. Multiplying the market risk premium by the security's beta indicates the amount of risk premium that needs to earned to adequately compensate the owner of a specific security for the market risk assumed. Adding the risk-free rate to this result gives the expected rate of return required to properly compensate the security owner for the use of its capital. If the security owner expects the security to return less than the CAPM amount, the security is probably overvalued, and the value of the stock could drop. If the owner's return expectation is higher than the CAPM amount, the security is probably undervalued and could increase in value.

4. Even though Investment A has a larger arithmetic average rate of return than Investment B, the geometric average rate of return is considered a better measurement of the rate of earnings because it considers the compounding effect of holding the investments over the ten-year period. The geometric average rates of return for the two investments are identical, so the investment can be chosen by considering the risk associated with each. Relative risk is best measured by comparing the coefficients of variation for the two investments. This metric measures the amount of variability in the rates of return relative to the average rate of return. For a risk-averse investor, Investment B is superior because the geometric average rate of return is no less than Investment A, and the relative volatility of the returns, as measured by the coefficient of variation, is less in Investment B. Therefore, Investment B provides the same rate of return at a lower level of risk.

Direct Your Learning

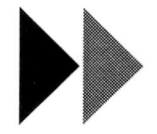

Assignment 11

Insurer Income and Dividend Policy

Educational Objectives

After learning the content of this assignment, you should be able to:

1. Describe the following measurements of income: accounting income, economic income, and market value compared with book value.
2. Describe the five components of total income and how they affect an insurer's income and policyholders' surplus.
3. Describe the requirements for a company to be taxed as an insurer for income tax purposes.
4. Explain the tax treatment of future liabilities of insurers.
5. Describe the types of state taxes that apply to insurers.
6. Explain the following with respect to shareholder dividends:
   - Reasons for dividends
   - Factors affecting insurance industry dividends
   - Alternatives to dividends
7. With respect to policyholder dividends:
   - Describe the financial effects
   - Explain the regulatory issues

Study Materials

Required Reading:
- Finance for Risk Management and Insurance Professionals
  - Chapter 11

Study Aids:
- SMART Online Practice Exams
- SMART Study Aids
  - Review Notes and Flash Cards—Assignment 11

Outline

▶ **Income Measurement in Financial Management**
  A. Accounting and Economic Income
    1. Accounting Income
    2. Economic Income
  B. Market Value Compared With Book Value
  C. Components of Insurer Income
    1. Underwriting Gain
    2. Net Investment Income
    3. Realized Capital Gains and Losses
    4. Unrealized Capital Gains and Losses
    5. Other Income

▶ **Income Tax Treatment**
  A. Requirements for Property-Casualty Insurer Tax Treatment
  B. Tax Rules for Property-Casualty Insurers
    1. Reserving for Future Liabilities
    2. Discounting of Future Liabilities
  C. State Taxation

▶ **Dividend Policy**
  A. Shareholder Dividends
    1. Reasons for Dividends
    2. Factors Affecting Insurance Industry Dividend Decisions
    3. Alternatives to Dividend Distributions
  B. Policyholder Dividends

▶ **Summary**

study tips: Before starting a new assignment, briefly review the Educational Objectives of those preceding it.

Key Words and Phrases

Define or describe each of the words and phrases listed below.

Accounting income (p. 11.4)

Economic income (p. 11.5)

Lintner model (p. 11.19)

Payout ratio (p. 11.19)

Review Questions

1. Describe how insurers' income is measured. (p. 11.3)

2. Explain how a company's income measurement rules and allocation methods complicate the measurement of income.
(pp. 11.3–11.4)

3. Describe how accounting income and economic income differ.
   (pp. 11.4–11.5)

4. Contrast the focus of generally accepted accounting principles (GAAP) and statutory accounting principles (SAP) regarding the treatment of income. (p. 11.4)

5. Identify difficulties that may occur in gauging the true value of a company when using only accounting income. (pp. 11.5–11.6)

6. List the four basic measurement standards emphasized by accounting. (p. 11.6)

7. Contrast the book value of a company with the market value of a company, and describe how each is calculated. (p. 11.6)

8. Describe the five components of an insurer's income. (pp. 11.7–11.13)

9. List two main sources of investable income for insurers. (p. 11.8)

10. Explain how it is possible for an insurer to maintain positive cash flows without earning a profit on underwriting. (p. 11.9)

11. Identify factors that limit an insurer's ability to raise its insurance leverage ratio and continue to increase the new business it writes. (p. 11.11)

12. Describe the effect of high inflation and interest rates on insurer portfolio management. (p. 11.12)

13. Describe the IRS definition of an insurer for federal tax purposes. (p. 11.14)

14. List the activities that the Internal Revenue Code (IRC) acknowledges as insurance activities. (p. 11.14)

15. List the general tax-rule areas applied to property-casualty insurers and noninsurers. (p. 11.15)

16. Identify differences in the tax treatment of income for property-casualty insurers and noninsurers. (p. 11.15)

17. Identify the event that triggers the deduction of estimates for unpaid losses for both reported and incurred but not reported losses. (p. 11.15)

18. List the two factors used as a basis for the industry discount rate published by the IRS. (p. 11.16)

19. Identify state taxes commonly levied on insurers. (p. 11.16)

20. Identify how a company might use after-tax income. (p. 11.17)

21. Contrast dividend policy decision-making as a financing decision and as an investment decision. (p. 11.18)

22. Identify a popular reason for increasing cash dividend payments to stockholders. (p. 11.18)

23. List two common alternatives to dividends as a way to distribute income to company owners. (p. 11.20)

24. Explain how policyholder dividends exhibit elements of both pricing adjustments and earnings distributions. (p. 11.21)

Application Questions

1. The goal of financial management is to maximize the market value of the company and thereby to maximize shareholders' wealth. The book value of the company, which is generated from the accounting records, is not the same as the company's market value. Explain the simplifying assumption that allows managers to use accounting income and wealth measurements in setting corporate goals.

2. CW Insurance Company wants to implement an aggressive growth strategy. In addition to the initial capital requirements of such a strategy, what factors should CW consider before implementing this strategy?

3. Unrealized gains and losses are not normally included in an insurer's net income. Explain how they may still have a significant effect on an insurer's policyholders' surplus and therefore on its business operations.

4. Dividends can sometimes be considered an investment decision. This means that, rather than reinvesting the money in the company, it is being paid out to the owners as compensation for the use of their capital. Explain the implications to the company of dividends paid as an investment decision.

Answers to Assignment 11 Questions

NOTE: These answers are provided to give students a basic understanding of acceptable types of responses. They often are not the only valid answers and are not intended to provide an exhaustive response to the questions.

Review Questions

1. An insurer's income is measured as the increase in net worth that a company generates during a specific period.

2. A company's income measurement rules must address the issue of how to allocate changes in the value of goods or services to arbitrary periods. The existence of more than one method for making allocations makes it difficult to consistently measure income.

3. Accounting income is the income for an accounting period determined by the application of a particular set of accounting rules to an organization's financial events. Economic income differs from accounting income because it depends on the market effects of the firm's economic activities and not just on the accounting income measurement rules that are used.

    Economic income is the change in a company's net worth during a particular period.

4. Treatment of income according to generally accepted accounting principles (GAAP) is based on measuring the company as a going concern. Treatment of income according to statutory accounting principles (SAP) is used for solvency regulation and is based on rules that assume the company will be liquidated.

5. The following difficulties may occur when gauging the true value of a company using only accounting income:
    - Accounting statements cannot accurately measure value changes.
    - Accounting income measurement can result in an artificial inflation of income figures.

6. The four basic measurement standards emphasized by accounting are:
    (1) Relevance
    (2) Verification
    (3) Freedom from bias
    (4) Quantifiability

7. The value of a company per its accounting records (its book value) is its value based on accounting income, calculated as the difference between revenues and costs (including taxes).

    The value of a company from the perspective of shareholders (its market value) is based on economic income and equals the dividends they receive plus changes in the market value of their shares.

8. The following are five components of an insurer's income:
    (1) Underwriting gain (UG)—Occurs if premiums earned in an accounting period exceed losses incurred (including loss adjustment expenses) and underwriting expenses incurred
    (2) Net investment income (NII)—Interest, dividends, and real estate income earned on invested assets minus expenses incurred in conducting investment operations

(3) Realized capital gains and losses (RCG)—Gain or loss that occurs when an insurer sells a capital asset for more or less than the cost of the asset

(4) Unrealized capital gains and losses (UCG)—Created by any appreciation or depreciation on bonds that do not qualify for amortized cost valuation and all equities

(5) Other income (OI)—Revenues and expenses that are not related to either underwriting or investment activities but are included in an insurer's net income

9. The following are two main sources of investable funds for insurers:
   (1) Capital and policyholders' surplus
   (2) Policyholder-supplied funds

10. It is possible for an insurer to maintain positive cash flows without earning a profit on underwriting because of timing differences between cash receipts and disbursements and between revenue and expense recognition.

11. The following factors limit an insurer's ability to raise its insurance leverage ratio and continue to increase the new business it writes:
    - The immediate recognition of underwriting expenses and deferral of revenues under statutory accounting reduces statutory net worth
    - Expected decline in profit margin as new business is written
    - Physical requirements involved in underwriting and otherwise servicing new business

12. High inflation and interest rates adversely affect insurer portfolio management by increasing underwriting cash needs and depressing the market values of existing bonds and mortgages.

13. The IRS definition of an insurer for federal tax purposes requires a company to issue insurance or annuity contracts, or reinsure risks underwritten by insurance companies, as more than 50 percent of its business during the taxable year. Once a company meets the definition of an insurer, it must determine whether it is a life insurer or a nonlife insurer.

14. The following activities are generally acknowledged as insurance activities:
    - Those that shift a risk of loss from an insured to an insurer (transfer)
    - Those that distribute risks among many insureds (sharing)
    - Those that involve an insurance contract (distribution by contract)

15. The general tax rule areas applied to property-casualty insurers and noninsurers include tax rates, depreciation, tax credits and carryovers, and employee benefits.

16. The following are differences in tax treatment of income for property-casualty insurers and noninsurers:
    - The ability of a property-casualty insurer to deduct the estimated amount of future liabilities regarding losses that have occurred.
    - The amounts of future obligations reported on the property-casualty insurer's Annual Statement must be discounted to present value for income tax purposes.

17. The occurrence of the loss is the triggering event for the deduction of estimates for unpaid losses for both reported and incurred but not reported losses.

18. The following two factors are used as a basis for the industry discount rate:
    (1) The interest rate that is determined annually by the IRS
    (2) Loss and adjustment expense payment patterns

19. In addition to income taxes, the following are state taxes commonly levied on insurers:
    - Gross premium tax
    - Fire marshal tax
    - Fire department tax
    - Guaranty fund
    - Workers' compensation funds

20. The after-tax income of a company may be used for the following purposes:
    - To purchase assets to help it expand its operations
    - To pay down debt
    - To invest in external investment opportunities
    - To pay out to the owners in the form of dividends

21. Companies that can efficiently secure additional equity capital should view dividend policy as a financing decision; otherwise, they should view it as an investment decision. If dividend policy is a financing decision, companies are not forced to forgo investment projects to pay dividends. If it is an investment decision, paying a dividend signals that management has not identified a sufficient number of opportunities on which the expected rate of return is at least equal to the company's own cost of capital to justify making external investments instead of paying dividends.

22. A popular reason for increasing cash dividend payments to stockholders is management's belief that higher dividends will create higher market prices for the company's shares.

23. Two common alternatives to dividends are:
    (1) Repurchasing corporate stock
    (2) Acquiring other companies

24. Policyholder dividends exhibit elements of both pricing adjustments and earnings distributions. For a stock insurer, a policyholder dividend should be regarded as an adjustment in the price of insurance, reflected in the practice of deducting policyholder dividends when determining the company's net underwriting gain, its taxable income, and its loss ratio and combined ratio.

    Because a mutual insurer does not have shareholders, the policyholder dividends can represent both a price adjustment factor and a dividend (earnings distribution). However, insurance accounting and tax accounting both treat dividends as an adjustment in the price of insurance.

Application Questions

1. The simplifying assumption that allows managers to use accounting income and wealth measurements in setting corporate goals is that changes in book value will be reflected in the market value of a company's stock. For example, if the value of a company's stock is equal to fifteen times the net income per share, every dollar of additional net income earned by the company is likely to increase the market value of the company by $15. This assumption allows managers to expect that a particular decision will have a similar effect on economic income and market value as it does on accounting income and book value.

2. Additional factors CW should consider before implementing an aggressive growth strategy include the effect of statutory accounting rules regarding the recognition of income and expenses on its policyholders' surplus during times of significant growth; the likely decline of profit margins as additional new business is written and losses increase; and the physical requirements, including labor, space, and equipment, of underwriting, processing, and servicing the new business.

3. Unrealized gains and losses are not normally included in an insurer's net income. However, they are included in an insurer's policyholders' surplus. Therefore, if CW has a significant portion of its investment portfolio in equities that are currently valued below their cost, the reduction in the value of the securities will reduce CW's policyholders' surplus. In the short term, a decline in policyholders' surplus can result in CW's insurance leverage ratio reaching an undesirable level and perhaps threaten its solvency. At a minimum, if policyholders' surplus is not restored, unrealized capital losses can force CW to accept a slower rate of growth than the one that was originally targeted.

4. If a dividend decision is an investment decision, then paying a dividend signals that management has not identified a sufficient number of opportunities on which the expected rate of return is at least equal to the company's own cost of capital to justify making investments instead of paying dividends. If management continues to be unable to find investments with acceptable returns, paying out dividends over time will lead to stagnation in the company's market value.

Direct Your Learning

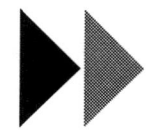

Assignment 12

Insurer Capital: Needs and Sources

Educational Objectives

After learning the content of this assignment, you should be able to:

1. Explain why insurers need adequate capital.

2. Explain how the following methods are used to meet insurers' internal capital needs:
   - Risk reduction
   - Operations
   - Balance sheet values

3. Explain how and why the following are used to provide external capital to insurers:
   - Equity
   - Mutual insurer reorganizations
   - Long-term debt
   - Alternative sources of capital

Study Materials

Required Reading:
- Finance for Risk Management and Insurance Professionals
  - Chapter 12

Study Aids:
- SMART Online Practice Exams
- SMART Study Aids
  - Review Notes and Flash Cards—Assignment 12

Outline

▶ **Insurer Capital Needs**

▶ **Internal Methods Used to Meet Capital Needs**
   A. Risk Reduction
      1. Increase Large Line Capacity
      2. Provide Catastrophe Protection
      3. Facilitate Withdrawal From a Market Segment
   B. Operations
      1. Net Income
      2. Surplus Relief
   C. Balance Sheet Values
      1. Loss Reserve Valuations
      2. Recognizing Existing Asset Market Values

▶ **External Methods Used to Meet Capital Needs**
   A. Equity
   B. Mutual Insurer Reorganization
      1. Demutualization
      2. Mutual Holding Company Conversion
   C. Long-Term Debt
   D. Alternative Sources of Capital
      1. Insurance-Linked Securities
      2. Contingent Capital Arrangements

▶ **Summary**

study tips: Perform a final review before your exam, but don't cram. Give yourself between two and four hours to go over the course work.

Key Words and Phrases
Define or describe each of the words and phrases listed below.

Risk-based capital (RBC) (p. 12.4)

Total adjusted capital (p. 12.4)

Authorized control level risk-based capital (ACL) (p. 12.4)

Reinsurance (p. 12.5)

Large line capacity (p. 12.6)

Ceding commission (p. 12.9)

Surplus relief (p. 12.10)

Finite risk reinsurance (p. 12.10)

Sale and leaseback (p. 12.12)

Surplus note (p. 12.17)

Review Questions

1. Explain why an insurer needs additional capital beyond its initial capital. (p. 12.3)

2. Describe the regulatory requirements regarding the capital needed by insurers. (p. 12.4)

3. Describe four major categories of risk that must be measured to determine the amount of an insurer's overall risk-based capital (RBC). (p. 12.4)

4. Describe the implications if an insurer fails to meet the RBC requirements. (p. 12.4)

5. Explain how insurers use risk reduction as a method to meet their internal capital needs. (p. 12.5)

6. Describe why insurers use reinsurance in risk reduction. (p. 12.5)

7. Explain how insurers can use reinsurance, in addition to risk reduction, to limit their need for additional capital. (pp. 12.5–12.7)

8. Explain how insurers use operations as a method to meet their internal capital needs. (pp. 12.7–12.10)

9. Describe how long-tail liability claims generate investment income for insurers. (p. 12.8)

10. Describe when insurers must recognize expenses and revenues for accounting purposes, according to state regulations. (p. 12.9)

11. Explain how the accounting rules for the recognition of insurer expenses and revenues affect policyholders' surplus. (p. 12.9)

12. Explain how reinsurance ceding commissions provide surplus relief. (p. 12.10)

13. Identify the two FAS 113 requirements necessary for a short-duration reinsurance transaction to qualify for reinsurance accounting treatment. (p. 12.11)

14. Describe how FAS 113 defines "insurance risk." (p. 12.11)

15. Explain how insurers use balance sheet values as a method of meeting their internal capital needs. (pp. 12.11–12.12)

16. Describe how changes to loss adjustment and loss adjustment expense reserves affect policyholders' surplus. (p. 12.12)

17. Describe how insurers use existing assets to increase asset values. (p. 12.12)

18. Explain how insurers use equity as a method to meet their external capital needs. (p. 12.13)

19. Explain why a mutual insurer might consider reorganization. (p. 12.13)

20. Identify two ways in which a mutual insurer can demutualize. (p. 12.14)

21. Describe what happens to a mutual insurer's surplus when the insurer demutualizes and becomes a stock insurer. (p. 12.14)

22. Explain how demutualization provides financial flexibility for an insurer. (p. 12.15)

23. Describe how demutualization provides organizational flexibility for an insurer. (p. 12.15)

24. Identify the disadvantages of demutualization. (p. 12.15)

25. Describe how insurers use long-term debt as a method to meet their external capital needs. (p. 12.17)

26. Identify the main method that mutual insurers use to raise surplus or equity. (p. 12.17)

27. Identify the two main categories of alternative sources of capital that insurers can use as a method to meet their external capital needs. (p. 12.19)

28. Explain how insurance-linked securities, such as catastrophe bonds, provide funds to help insurers offset catastrophe losses. (p. 12.19)

29. Describe how insurers can use contingent capital arrangements as a method to meet their external capital needs. (p. 12.21)

30. Describe how contingent capital can be provided. (p. 12.21)

31. Explain how the investors of contingent surplus notes (CSN) are compensated for providing standby funds to the insurer and for taking on the notes' credit risk. (p. 12.21)

32. Explain how insurers can use catastrophe equity put options to raise funds in the event of catastrophe losses. (p. 12.22)

33. Identify a major benefit of catastrophe equity put options. (p. 12.23)

Application Questions

1. A property-casualty insurer has total adjusted capital of $15 million. The company's authorized control level risk-based capital, as determined by using the risk-based capital formula, is $11.5 million. Referring to the risk-based capital requirements, identify what level of regulatory action the company will be subject to, and explain what the ramifications are to the company.

2. A property-casualty insurer has decided that writing medical malpractice no longer fits into the company's strategic plan and that it will withdraw from the market. The company wants to limit the amount of capital it must allocate to the withdrawal from the market. Identify and explain the advantages and disadvantages of each option available to the company.

3. A property-casualty insurer is experiencing substantial premium growth because of an extremely effective marketing campaign. This rapid growth is creating a drain on policyholders' surplus because of the mismatch when recording premium revenues and expenses under statutory accounting rules. Explain how reinsurance can be used to create surplus relief.

4. A property-casualty insurer has decided to issue catastrophe bonds to provide capital for losses related to hurricanes in the Southeast. From an investor's perspective, what are three insurance-related risks of this type of investment beyond the risk of a hurricane itself?

Answers to Assignment 12 Questions

NOTE: These answers are provided to give students a basic understanding of acceptable types of responses. They often are not the only valid answers and are not intended to provide an exhaustive response to the questions.

Review Questions

1. Additional capital is needed to pay for expanded sales and operational capabilities such as marketing and advertising expenses, new employees and related expenses, and additional information technology resources. Also, as the amount of insurance written increases, the insurer will need more capital to provide a larger reserve to cover unexpected losses. Additional capital is also needed to replenish policyholders' surplus for the reduction in net income caused by statutory accounting rules that require insurers to recognize all policy acquisition costs at the time the policy is written (as opposed to ratably over the policy period in the way that premium revenue is recognized).

2. An insurer must meet certain regulatory requirements regarding the amount of its capital and policyholders' surplus. The minimum amount of initial capital required for an insurer is set by the state in which it is domiciled. This amount depends on the type of business organization the insurer uses, generally either stock or mutual, and the lines of business the insurer writes. The amounts vary by state statute, from $150,000 to $5 million. However, the ongoing amount of capital required depends on the amount of the insurer's risk-based capital.

3. The four major categories of risk that must be measured to arrive at an insurer's overall risk-based capital (RBC) amount are as follows:

    (1) Asset risk—A measure of an asset's default risk on principal or decline in market value as a result of changes in the market

    (2) Credit risk—A measure of the default risk on amounts that are due from policyholders, reinsurers, or creditors

    (3) Underwriting risk—A measure of the risk that arises from underestimating the liabilities from business already written or inadequately pricing current or prospective business

    (4) Business risk—A measure of the risk caused by excessive rates of growth, contingent liabilities, or other items not reflected on the balance sheet

4. An insurer's failure to meet the RBC requirements can lead to the following four levels of regulatory action, depending on the amount of the shortfall:

    (1) At the company-action level, which is when the insurer's total adjusted capital is less than 200 percent of the authorized control level risk-based capital (ACL), the insurer is required to submit a business plan to regulators indicating how RBC requirements will be met in the future.

    (2) At the regulatory-control level, which is when the insurer's total adjusted capital is less than 150 percent of the ACL, additional regulatory involvement may be initiated.

    (3) At the authorized-control level, which is when the insurer's total adjusted capital is less than 100 percent of the ACL, regulators may take control of the insurer.

    (4) If the insurer's total adjusted capital is less than 70 percent of the ACL, regulators are required to take control of the insurer.

5. As an alternative to raising additional capital, an insurer may seek to reduce the amount of capital required by reducing its overall exposure to risks. For example, if the cost of obtaining additional capital for writing more insurance exceeds the profits projected from that business, then reducing capital requirements may ultimately generate a higher rate of return to the owners.

6. The main purpose of reinsurance is to stabilize a primary insurer's loss experience. Smoothing the peaks and troughs of loss experience is important because an insurer must have a reasonably steady flow of profits to attract and retain capital to support growth.

7. Insurers can use reinsurance to limit their need for additional capital in the following ways:
   - To increase large line capacity: Reinsurers can provide primary insurers with large line capacity by accepting liability for those high-value loss exposures that the primary insurer would otherwise be unwilling or unable to accept. Purchasing reinsurance enables the primary insurer to increase its market share without having to increase its capital.
   - To provide catastrophe protection: Insurers can also use reinsurance to protect themselves from the financial consequences of a single catastrophic event causing multiple losses. Both natural and man-made catastrophes can result in significant property and liability losses. The use of reinsurance would provide stability to the insurer's financial position in case of an unexpected catastrophe, allowing the insurer to reduce the amount of capital it must have available.
   - To facilitate withdrawal from a market segment: A primary insurer may determine that a particular market segment no longer fits into its business strategy or will not be profitable in the future; therefore, it may want to withdraw from that market segment. Portfolio reinsurance might be an attractive option to facilitate such a withdrawal. Portfolio reinsurance reinsures groupings (portfolios) of loss exposures of an entire type of insurance, class of business, or geographic area. Portfolio reinsurance can allow a primary insurer to identify and limit the amount of capital it will need to allocate to the market from which it is withdrawing.

8. The most valuable source of internal capital is the generation of net income from the insurer's business operations. An insurer's business operations raise capital from the premiums received when insurance policies are sold. In some cases, internal capital can also come from surplus relief provided by reinsurance transactions.

9. It can be many years before long-tail liability claims become known to the insured, are officially reported as claims, and are finalized and paid. In effect, long-tail claims create long-term debt, the proceeds of which become part of the insurer's investment portfolio and are used to generate investment income and increase policyholders' surplus. However, long-term debt is not considered capital for regulatory purposes.

10. State insurance regulation mandates that for accounting purposes, all expenses related to the acquisition (sale) of an insurance policy be recognized at the time the policy is sold. However, insurance accounting rules also require the insurer to recognize premiums as revenue only as they are earned over the policy's life.

11. Immediately recognizing expenses combined with gradually recognizing revenue causes an insurer's policyholders' surplus to decrease.

12. Ceding commissions are usually a percentage of the ceded written premiums and are recognized as revenue by the primary insurer at the time the reinsurance is put into effect. Therefore, both revenue and policyholders' surplus increase. Consequently, the reinsurance transaction provides surplus relief.

13. According to FAS 113, a short-duration reinsurance transaction qualifies for reinsurance accounting treatment only if the following two requirements are met:
    (1) The reinsurer assumes significant insurance risk under the reinsured portions of the underlying insurance contracts.
    (2) It is reasonably possible that the reinsurer may realize a significant loss from the transaction.

14. FAS 113 defines "insurance risk" as including both underwriting risk and timing risk. Underwriting risk is described as the uncertainty about the ultimate amount of any premiums, commissions, claims, and claim settlement expenses. Timing risk is described as the uncertainty about the timing of premiums, commissions, claims, and claim settlement expenses.

15. The following two types of activities are commonly used to provide capital on a balance sheet:
    (1) Actions to change loss and loss adjustment expense reserve valuations
    (2) Transactions that recognize existing asset market values

16. Any adjustments reducing loss reserves will reduce loss expenses in the year the adjustment is made, thereby increasing both net income and policyholders' surplus. Any adjustments made to increase reserves will decrease net income and policyholders' surplus.

17. Insurers can use existing assets to increase asset value by sale and leaseback transactions, through which the owner of an asset sells the asset to another party and then leases the asset back from the new owner. Because the sold asset was previously carried on the insurer's balance sheet at historical cost, the difference between fair market value and historical cost was not included in the insurer's capital. However, when the asset was sold, the entire proceeds of the sale became an admitted asset. Therefore, the difference between historical cost and higher fair market value (minus taxes due on the gain from the sale) is now included in the insurer's capital, thereby increasing the capital.

18. Insurers organized as stock companies have the option of using the capital markets to raise equity capital, based on their particular capital needs and financial circumstances. However, mutual insurers do not have the option to access the capital markets to raise equity capital because they are owned by their policyholders.

19. The inability of a mutual insurer to use the financial markets to raise capital can limit its strategic options, such as those related to mergers and acquisitions. Therefore, a mutual insurer may determine that the stock form of ownership will provide it with more flexibility and alternatives for raising capital.

20. A mutual insurer can demutualize in two ways. It can go through a complete demutualization process into a stock company, or it can go through a mutual holding company conversion.

21. When a mutual company demutualizes and becomes a stock company, the insurer's surplus is usually distributed to policyholders as stock, cash, and policy enhancements. Most policyholders will receive stock, but some will receive cash or policy enhancements that have an equivalent value.

22. Demutualization provides financial flexibility because the reorganized company can issue stock and debt and can obtain bank credit facilities. It provides maximum access to capital to finance future growth, and it creates a source of payment that the company can use for mergers and acquisitions.

23. Demutualization provides organizational flexibility because business entities can become subsidiaries of a holding company rather than the insurer, thereby simplifying insurer regulation. Also, offering stock options can help to attract and retain employees.

24. One disadvantage of demutualization is that the demutualization process is very expensive. Ongoing administration is also expensive because of the increased financial reporting requirements of publicly traded companies and because the company is likely to have many small shareholders. The process is also time consuming; it can take from eighteen to twenty-four months to complete. During this time, management's attention is distracted from other duties.

25. Insurers can use long-term debt to meet their external capital needs by selling bonds to raise long-term debt capital.

26. Surplus notes are the main method mutual insurers use to raise surplus or equity.

27. The two main categories of alternative sources of capital that insurers can use to meet their external capital needs are insurance-linked securities, which in effect are direct risk transfer instruments, and contingent capital securities, which reduce an insurer's need for traditional sources of capital.

28. Insurance-linked securities provide funds to help offset the catastrophe losses suffered by an insurer. They do this by transferring the risk of loss from a catastrophe directly to the investor. Catastrophe bonds are the most commonly used insurance-linked security. Insurers issue catastrophe bonds to the providers of capital with the provision that the payment of interest, repayment of principal, or both are reduced or even eliminated in the event of a specified catastrophe. Therefore, the investor in the bond assumes the risk that a catastrophe will occur. The insurer uses the reduction or elimination of interest payments and principal repayments to offset the losses from the catastrophe.

29. Contingent capital arrangements are agreements entered into before any losses occur, and they enable an insurer to raise cash by selling stock or issuing debt at prearranged terms. The insurer pays a capital commitment fee to the party that agrees in advance to buy the equity or debt securities following a loss. Using a contingent capital arrangement does not transfer the insurer's risk of loss to the investors. However, after a loss occurs, the insurer receives an inflow of capital to replenish its policyholders' surplus after it pays for the loss.

30. Contingent capital can be provided through a contingent surplus note arrangement or through the purchase of a catastrophe equity put option. Contingent surplus notes are prearranged to allow an insurer, at its option, to immediately obtain funds by issuing surplus notes at a pre-agreed rate and maturity. Contingent surplus notes are made available to an insurer through a contingent surplus note (CSN) trust, which receives funds from investors and places them in liquid investments such as U.S. Treasury securities. In exchange, the investors receive trust notes from the CSN trust. For a specified time, the insurer can, at its option, receive the cash value of the trust investments in exchange for surplus notes that it issues to the trust. Therefore, the insurer has a standby source of cash that it can use to help it recover from large losses.

31. As compensation for providing standby funds to the insurer and taking the credit risk involved with any surplus notes that are issued, the investors in the CSN trust receive a return higher than that available from other liquid investments of comparable maturity.

32. Insurers use catastrophe equity put options (also called catastrophe equity puts) to raise funds in the event of catastrophic losses. A catastrophe equity put option is the right to sell equity (stock) at a predetermined price in the event of a catastrophic loss. The purchaser of a catastrophe equity put option pays a commitment fee to the seller for the seller's commitment to purchase the equity at a pre-agreed price in the event of a catastrophic loss, as defined in the put agreement.

33. A major benefit of catastrophe equity put options is that they make equity capital available at a pre-agreed price immediately after a catastrophe, when the insurer most needs that capital. If an insurer suffers a loss of capital as a result of a catastrophe, its stock price is likely to decrease, lowering the amount it would receive from newly issued stock. Catastrophe put options provide instant equity at a predetermined price to help an insurer replenish its capital following such a loss.

Application Questions

1. Because the insurer's total adjusted capital is less than 150 percent of its authorized control level risk-based capital ($15,000,000 ÷ 11,500,000 = 130%), it is subject to the regulatory-control level requirements. At this level, the company is required to submit a business plan to regulators, indicating how the RBC requirements will be met in the future. In addition, regulators are authorized to initiate additional regulatory involvement if they deem it necessary.

2. An insurer that wants to limit the capital it must allocate to a market from which it is withdrawing, has the following options:
    - It can simply stop selling new insurance policies and continue serving the existing in-force policies until they all expire. Under this option, the company continues to expose its capital to the risk in a market from which it wants to withdraw.
    - It can cancel all policies, if allowed by regulators, and refund all unearned premium. This could expose the company and its capital to reputational risk from not fulfilling its original promises under the insurance contracts that were issued.
    - It can purchase reinsurance to be indemnified for all losses incurred as of and following the date of the reinsurance agreement. Although this type of reinsurance is expensive, it allows the insurer to the limit the amount of capital it has exposed to the market from which it is withdrawing.

3. If a primary insurer reinsures certain loss exposures, the primary insurer may receive a ceding commission from the reinsurer on those loss exposures ceded. The purpose of the ceding commission is to cover all or part of the primary insurer's policy acquisition expenses. The ceding commission is usually a percentage of the ceded written premiums, and it is recognized as revenue by the primary insurer at the time the reinsurance is put into effect. Therefore, both the primary insurer's revenue and policyholders' surplus are increased. Consequently, the reinsurance transaction provides surplus relief.

4. In addition to the direct risk of losses because of the occurrence of a hurricane, the investors in hurricane catastrophe bonds may be subject to other risks because the insurer knows it has additional capital available to cover hurricane losses. These added risks include the following:
    - The insurer may relax its underwriting guidelines.
    - The insurer may be less stringent about managing geographic concentration of exposures.
    - The insurer may be willing to be more liberal when settling claims.

Direct Your Learning

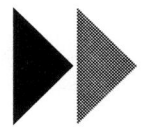

Capital Structure of Insurers

Educational Objectives

After learning the content of this assignment, you should be able to:

1. Describe the components of a typical capital structure for a corporation.
2. Explain how companies apply financial leverage to increase returns to shareholders.
3. Given appropriate data, calculate the cost of equity using the following methods:
   - Dividend growth model
   - Capital asset pricing model (CAPM)
   - Security market line (SML)
4. Explain how an insurer determines its cost of debt from bonds and insurance operations.
5. Given appropriate data, calculate the cost of preferred stock.
6. Given appropriate data, calculate the weighted average cost of capital for an insurer.
7. Explain how general factors and specific insurance-related factors affect the optimal capital structure of an insurer.
8. Explain how an insurer's capital structure affects its valuation.

Study Materials

Required Reading:
- Finance for Risk Management and Insurance Professionals
  - Chapter 13

Study Aids:
- SMART Online Practice Exams
- SMART Study Aids
  - Review Notes and Flash Cards—Assignment 13

ASSIGNMENT 13

Outline

- **Typical Capital Structure**
    - A. Equity
    - B. Debt
    - C. Financial Leverage
        1. Financial Leverage Analysis
        2. Degree of Financial Leverage
- **Insurer Capital**
    - A. Cost of Equity
        1. Dividend Growth Model
        2. Capital Asset Pricing Model (CAPM)
        3. Security Market Line (SML)
    - B. Cost of Debt
    - C. Cost of Preferred Stock
    - D. Weighted Average Cost of Capital
- **Optimal Capital Structure**
    - A. Tax Shield
    - B. Cost of Financial Distress
    - C. Agency Costs
    - D. Asymmetric Information
- **Optimal Capital Structure for Insurers**
    - A. Factors Affecting an Insurer's Market Value
    - B. Ownership
    - C. Effects of Capital Structure on Insurer Valuation
- **Summary**

When reviewing for your exam, remember to allot time for frequent breaks.

Key Words and Phrases

Define or describe each of the words and phrases listed below.

Financial leverage (p. 13.5)

Degree of financial leverage (p. 13.8)

Cost of capital (p. 13.10)

Cost of equity (p. 13.11)

Cost of debt (p. 13.15)

Weighted average cost of capital (WACC) (p. 13.17)

Tax shield (p. 13.18)

Agency costs (p. 13.19)

Asymmetric information theory (p. 13.20)

Review Questions

1. Explain how a company's funds flow in a cycle. (p. 13.3)

2. Describe the debt and equity features of preferred stock. (p. 13.4)

3. Explain why preferred stock might be converted to common stock. (p. 13.4)

4. Explain how debt capital is usually raised. (p. 13.5)

5. Explain how debt is used to increase returns to shareholders. (p. 13.5)

6. Describe financial leverage analysis. (p. 13.5)

7. Contrast the degree of financial leverage with the debt-to-equity ratio. (p. 13.10)

8. Explain why insurers require capital in addition to the capital required to invest in real assets. (p. 13.10)

9. Describe the other functions of insurer capital in addition to investing in real assets and moderating the volatility of the insurance portfolio. (p. 13.10)

10. Identify three approaches for estimating the cost of equity capital. (p. 13.11)

11. Explain how the cost of debt is similar to the cost of equity. (p. 13.15)

12. Identify the two steps for determining the cost of debt for new issues. (p. 13.15)

13. Describe one way insurers can approximate the cost of debt created by writing insurance policies. (p. 13.16)

14. Explain why investment projects that have an expected rate of return greater than a company's WACC will create positive net present value for the company. (p. 13.17)

15. Describe the optimal capital structure of a company. (p. 13.18)

16. Explain what the Modigliani and Miller (M&M) proposition suggests about financial leverage. (p. 13.18)

17. Identify the factors that affect the ability of models, such as the Modigliani and Miller (M&M) proposition, to accurately predict the effect of financial leverage decisions. (p. 13.18)

18. Describe the effect of a rising ratio of debt to equity. (p. 13.19)

19. Identify the positive and negative effect of increasing financial leverage. (p. 13.19)

20. Identify the three categories of agency costs. (p. 13.19)

21. Explain how the asymmetric information theory affects the determination of an optimal capital structure. (p. 13.20)

22. Identify the essential issue for insurers about their optimal capital structure. (p. 13.21)

23. Identify three significant factors capital markets use to value securities. (p. 13.21)

24. Explain how an insurer's form of ownership affects its capital structure decisions. (p. 13.22)

25. Explain the effect that capital structure can have on the company's valuation. (pp. 13.22–13.23)

26. Explain why policyholders, agents and brokers, and regulatory agencies have an incentive to monitor insurer financial health. (p. 13.23)

Application Questions

1. CW Insurance Company, a stock insurer, needs to raise capital to implement its new growth strategy. CW's financial manager must raise the new capital from the source that will provide the greatest increase in wealth for the existing owners. Assuming the amount of capital to be raised will not affect CW's credit rating, would the financial manager raise the capital from the sale of common stock or bonds? Why?

2. Using the dividend growth model, determine the cost of equity for CW Insurance Company. CW's common stock is currently selling for $75.00 per share and is paying a $2.25 annual dividend. Dividends are expected to grow at 7 percent per year for the foreseeable future.

3. If CW is considering raising its new capital from the sale of bonds, it will need to know its before-tax and after-tax cost of debt. Other debt instruments with equivalent credit risk and maturity have a current yield to maturity of 8.5 percent. Explain how CW can determine its pre-tax and after-tax cost of debt.

4. As part of CW's decision process for determining how to structure the new capital to be raised, four significant factors must be considered: taxes, financial distress, agency costs, and asymmetric information. Explain how each of these factors affects the cost of capital.

Answers to Assignment 13 Questions

NOTE: These answers are provided to give students a basic understanding of acceptable types of responses. They often are not the only valid answers and are not intended to provide an exhaustive response to the questions.

Review Questions

1. Company funds flow in the following cycle:
   - Company securities are sold to suppliers of capital in the capital markets.
   - Proceeds from the security's sale are used to purchase assets.
   - Cash returns from the assets can be retained in the company to finance operations or to finance the purchase of more assets.
   - Ultimately, cash returns can be distributed to the suppliers of capital.
   - Debt holders receive income in the form of interest payments, and equity holders can receive income as cash dividends.

2. Preferred stock has features of both debt and equity. It can resemble debt if its dividend is a fixed obligation (either a stated percentage of the par value of the preferred share or a stated dollar amount per share) and can resemble equity in that omission of a dividend does not result in the entire issue becoming payable immediately, as would a bond.

3. Some preferred stock, like some debt securities, is convertible into common stock under terms and conditions specified at the time of issue. This feature is used when the company wants to sell common stock to increase capital, but when selling is not economical because the company's stock price is depressed.

4. Debt capital is usually raised through the sale of bonds in the capital market.

5. Using fixed cost funds (debt) to increase returns to shareholders is called financial leverage. This increase is accomplished by using the capital raised by the issue of debt to earn a rate of return higher than the fixed costs of that debt.

6. Financial leverage analysis is a technique used to compare earnings per share (EPS) under alternate capitalization plans with varying levels of debt and equity.

7. The degree of financial leverage identifies the effect of a company's financial leverage on its earnings per share, whereas the debt-to-equity ratio indicates the amount of a company's financial leverage.

8. In addition to the capital required to invest in real assets, insurers require capital, or policyholders' surplus, to moderate the volatility in the insurance portfolio. If claim payments exceed projections, the insurer's equity capital must finance the shortfall in the short term. Over a longer term, premiums will be brought into balance with claims, and the company's policyholders' surplus will be restored.

9. In addition to serving the functions of investing in real assets and moderating the volatility of the insurance portfolio, insurer capital has several other functions. Insurer capital provides the financing for the creation and growth of the unearned premium, loss, and loss adjustment reserves required by statutory accounting rules as an insurer's premium volume increases. It also absorbs fluctuations in the value of the company's investment portfolio and in the gains and losses realized upon the sale of securities.

10. Three approaches for estimating the cost of equity capital are:
    (1) Dividend growth model
    (2) Capital asset pricing model (CAPM)
    (3) Security market line (SML)

11. Like the cost of equity, the cost of debt is essentially an opportunity cost concept that compares the return on insurer debt with the return on other debt of equivalent credit risk.

12. Determining the cost of debt for new issues is a two-step process. The first step determines the before-tax cost of debt. The second step is to adjust for taxes because bond interest is deductible for income tax purposes.

13. One way to approximate the cost of debt created by writing insurance policies is to use the cost of bonds with maturities similar to the duration of the reserves that are currently being issued by the insurer or by another company with equivalent credit risk to the insurer.

14. Investment projects that have an expected rate of return greater than the company's WACC will create positive net present value for the company because such investment projects should result in higher stock prices and therefore increase the wealth of the shareholders. Investment projects that are expected to earn less than the company's WACC will result in a decrease in shareholder value and should be avoided.

15. The optimal capital structure of a company is the combination of debt and equity capital at which the company continues to increase in value.

16. The Modigliani and Miller (M&M) proposition suggests that financial leverage has no effect on a company's cost of capital because the cost of capital depends not on how the company is financed but on the risk profile of the company itself compared with other companies. If the company issues more debt and its risk profile increases, the cost of equity capital will rise to offset the use of low-cost debt and thereby leave the overall cost of capital constant.

17. The factors that affect the ability of models, such as the Modigliani and Miller (M&M) proposition, to accurately predict the effect of financial leverage decisions are taxes, cost of financial distress, agency costs, and asymmetric information.

18. As the debt-to-equity ratio rises, a company will experience an increased risk of defaulting on its debt and an increased potential of bankruptcy. The owners of the securities issued by the company, who will bear the costs associated with these events, will also be assuming more risk as the company's use of debt equity continues to increase.

19. Increasing financial leverage has both a positive and a negative effect. The positive effect is that the tax shield increases the company's value. However, as leverage rises, so does the probability of bankruptcy. Therefore, the negative effect of increasing financial leverage equates to the present value of bankruptcy costs.

20. The three categories of agency costs are monitoring costs, bonding costs, and incentive alignment costs.

21. Asymmetric information theory holds that company managers prefer to finance projects first with internally generated funds. If internal funds are inadequate, external funds will be raised first from the issuance of bonds and then, only if necessary, from the issuance of new stock. The basis of this theory is that a company's financial managers have better information about the company's prospects than others and that they can better anticipate changes in the company's operating income.

22. The essential issue about the optimal capital structure for insurers is how much insurance should be written for a given amount of policyholders' surplus. The optimal capital structure for an insurer is to have enough capital to support writing policies that are expected to be profitable, up to the point at which the next policy written would begin causing the value of the company to decline.

23. Three significant factors used by the capital markets to value securities are earnings, risk, and growth.

24. Form of ownership affects insurers' capital structure decisions because it is commonly accepted that stock companies are under greater pressure to perform because of shareholder overview of their activities. Empirical analysis shows that stock companies are generally more highly leveraged than mutual insurers. Because mutual insurers are owned by their policyholders, they do not issue stock and therefore do not have access to the external capital that is available to stock insurers. Therefore, the optimal capital structure of a mutual insurer differs from that of a stock insurer because a mutual insurer's equity capital comes from the sale of insurance policies and the compensation to the policyholder owners is paid in the form of lower premiums.

25. The capital structure of an insurer can affect the company's valuation. Selling more insurance on a fixed dollar amount of equity or policyholders' surplus increases the expected return to the owners of the insurer, provided the spread is favorable. A favorable spread occurs when the cost of policyholder-supplied funds is less than the available rates of return on investments.

    As more policies are sold, the risk of default starts to rise but is still outweighed by the benefits of the spread. Eventually, the market perceives that the company's exposure, as measured by the written premium-to-surplus ratio, is so high that the cost of policyholder funds exceeds the rates of return available from investments and the company's value will decline if additional insurance is sold.

26. Policyholders have an incentive to monitor their insurers' solvency when they bear the costs of financial distress. For example, large corporate clients who do not receive protection from guarantee associations have an interest in monitoring their insurers' financial health. Agents and brokers also have an incentive to monitor company financial health. Excessive leverage can harm a company's rating and cause agents and brokers to send clients to safer companies. Regulatory agencies, as required by law, monitor insurer financial conditions for those companies within their jurisdiction. If leverage becomes too high, the regulator can instruct management to alter its policies, and management could lose control of the company to the regulator.

Application Questions

1. The goal of CW's financial manager is to increase the wealth of CW's existing owners. This means increasing the value of the currently outstanding shares of CW stock. A significant way to increase the value of the stock is to increase CW's earnings per share. Change in earnings per share amounts are reflected in the value of a stock. Therefore, if earnings per share increase, with no corresponding increase in the risk profile of CW, the value of CW's stock will increase. CW can create financial leverage by selling bonds to raise the capital needed to implement its growth strategy. A disadvantage of using debt capital is the potential for creating financial distress, such as committing to long-term liabilities and increasing the potential for bankruptcy. The fact that CW's capital structure will not result in a change in its credit rating indicates that increased financial distress issues will not be a problem. Based on the facts provided, CW's financial manager should raise the needed capital by issuing bonds.

2. The cost of equity for CW using the dividend growth model is calculated as follows:

$$V_0 = D_1 \div (r - g),$$

where:

V_0 = Value of stock

D_1 = Dividend at end of next period

g = Annual dividend growth

r = Market return for this stock (cost of equity)

By rearranging the formula to solve for r, the cost of equity can be calculated as follows:

$D_1 = \$2.41$ ($\$2.25 \times 1.07 = \$2.41$)

$$\begin{aligned}\text{Cost of equity} &= (D_1 \div V_0) + g \\ &= (\$2.41 \div \$75.00) + 0.07 \\ &= 0.032 + 0.07 \\ &= 0.102, \text{ or } 10.2\%.\end{aligned}$$

3. Determining the cost of debt for new issues of bonds is a two-step process. The first step determines the before-tax cost of debt. The before-tax cost of debt is the rate of interest required in the market, the yield to maturity, for bonds of that quality and maturity. This rate is required because if CW's new bonds don't provide for at least that yield, no investors will buy them. Therefore, CW's before-tax cost of debt must be 8.5 percent.

The second step is determining the after-tax cost of debt by adjusting the before-tax rate for income taxes because bond interest is deductible for income tax purposes. Assuming a 35 percent marginal tax rate (T), the after-tax cost of debt is as follows:

$$\begin{aligned}\text{After-tax cost of debt} &= i \times (1 - T) \\ &= 8.5 \times (1 - 0.35) \\ &= 5.53\%.\end{aligned}$$

4. Four of the most important factors when determining the overall capital structure of a company are taxes, financial distress, agency costs, and asymmetric information.

An advantage of debt capital is that interest paid on debt is deductible for income tax purposes, while dividends paid on stock are not. Therefore, the tax savings, or the tax shield, have the effect of reducing the company's weighted cost of capital.

The costs of financial distress increase as leverage rises, as does the probability of bankruptcy. Therefore, a negative effect of increasing financial leverage equates to the present value of bankruptcy costs. At low levels of debt, the cost of financial distress is also low. As the level of debt increases, the cost of financial distress increases until at some point it exceeds the value of the tax shield. Once the cost of financial distress is greater than the tax shield, the value of the company will start to decline. Therefore, management must carefully consider the maximum amount of financial leverage it can use before negatively affecting the value of the company and increasing its cost of capital.

Agency costs are the costs associated with the agency relationship between the owners and management of the company. As the number of shareholders increases, aligning the interests of company management and the shareholders becomes more difficult. Expenses involved in monitoring management's activities to ensure that they are in the best interests of the company are an additional direct cost to the owners, adding to the cost of equity. Another relationship that can add costs is the shareholder-bondholder relationship. After raising money from the sale of bonds, the company may enter riskier types of projects that might have high rates of return for the owners but not compensate the bondholders for the additional credit. However, bondholders understand this possibility and sometimes place restrictive covenants in the bonds. These covenants are meaningful only if they are enforced, which involves costs. These costs make the use of debt more expensive.

The theory of asymmetric information could decrease the cost of capital if investors assume new shares are issued only if they have unusually profitable investment opportunities that cannot be delayed and that cannot be financed with debt. Alternatively, it might be viewed that new shares should be issued only when management believes the company's stock is overvalued. Therefore, the sale of new shares would signal bad news to current shareholders. A bad-news signal will cause stock prices to drop, thereby increasing the company's cost of equity financing.

Direct Your Learning

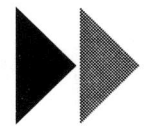

Assignment 14

Making Capital Investment Decisions

Educational Objectives

After learning the content of this assignment, you should be able to:

1. Given the appropriate financial information, determine the required rate of return for an investment.

2. Given appropriate data, apply the following capital investment evaluation techniques to identify an acceptable investment alternative:

   - Accounting rate of return
   - Payback rule
   - Breakeven analysis
   - Net present value
   - Internal rate of return

3. Given appropriate data, explain whether net present value or internal rate of return should be used when deciding whether to accept a project.

4. Describe soft and hard capital rationing.

5. Explain why underwriting insurance is a borrowing project.

6. Given appropriate data, determine premium needed to achieve a target underwriting profit.

Study Materials

Required Reading:
- Finance for Risk Management and Insurance Professionals
  - Chapter 14

Study Aids:
- SMART Online Practice Exams
- SMART Study Aids
  - Review Notes and Flash Cards—Assignment 14

Outline

▶ **Capital Budgeting Techniques**
  A. Required Rate of Return
  B. Capital Investment Evaluation Techniques
     1. Accounting Rate of Return
     2. Payback Rule
     3. Breakeven Analysis
  C. Discounted Cash Flow Techniques
     1. Net Present Value
     2. Internal Rate of Return
  D. Net Present Value Compared With Internal Rate of Return
     1. Lending Projects Compared With Borrowing Projects
     2. Multiple Rates of Return
     3. Mutually Exclusive Projects
  E. Capital Rationing
     1. Soft Rationing
     2. Hard Rationing
▶ **Insurance Policies as Borrowing Projects**
▶ **Target Underwriting Profit Margins**
▶ **Summary**

If you find your attention drifting, take a short break to regain your focus.

Key Words and Phrases

Define or describe each of the words and phrases listed below.

Accounting rate of return (p. 14.5)

Payback (p. 14.7)

Breakeven analysis (p. 14.8)

Net present value (*NPV*) (p. 14.11)

Internal rate of return (*IRR*) (p. 14.12)

Lending project (p. 14.13)

Borrowing project (p. 14.13)

Capital rationing (p. 14.17)

Soft rationing (p. 14.18)

Hard rationing (p. 14.18)

Review Questions

1. Describe the process used in making capital budgeting decisions. (p. 14.3)

2. Describe the discount rate used by the following entities when making financial allocation decisions:

    a. Investors (p. 14.4)

    b. Companies (p. 14.4)

3. Explain how to calculate the weighted average cost of capital. (p. 14.4)

4. Describe flotation costs, and explain why a company should consider them when making investment decisions. (p. 14.4)

5. Describe how the following capital investment evaluation strategies are used to analyze investment alternatives:
   a. Accounting rate of return (pp. 14.5–14.7)

   b. Payback rule (pp. 14.7–14.8)

   c. Breakeven analysis (pp. 14.8–14.10)

6. Identify the major flaw in using the accounting rate of return in assessing capital investment. (p. 14.7)

7. Describe the following costs used in capital investment breakeven analysis:
   a. Fixed costs (p. 14.9)

b. Profit per sales dollar (p. 14.9)

c. Variable costs (p. 14.9)

8. Explain how using accounting breakeven differs from using economic breakeven when evaluating investment alternatives. (pp. 14.9–14.10)

9. Describe how the following cash flow techniques are used to analyze investment alternatives:
   a. Net present value (NPV) (p. 14.11)

   b. Internal rate of return (IRR) (pp. 14.12–14.13)

10. Distinguish between a lending project and a borrowing project. (p. 14.13)

11. Describe situations in which the *IRR* and *NPV* rules could lead to ambiguous decisions regarding investment decisions. (pp. 14.13–14.17)

12. Differentiate the two forms of capital rationing used to limit a company's capital expenditures. (pp. 14.17–14.18)

13. List reasons why a company may have difficulty raising capital for investments. (p. 14.18)

14. Describe how an insurance contract follows the cash flow pattern of a borrowing project. (p. 14.19)

15. Explain how the discount rate affects an insurance policy's value to the insurance company. (p. 14.20)

16. Identify a possible use of capital budgeting by an insurer. (p. 14.20)

17. Identify sources of insurance company income used in an insurer's capital budgeting decisions in determining underwriting profit margins in insurance rates. (p. 14.21)

18. Describe how an insurer's investment income and underwriting profits are affected by the competitive market. (p. 14.23)

Application Questions

1. Assume KAO Enterprises has $1 million in shareholders' equity and $1.5 million in debt. KAO's common stock returns 12 percent, and its debt returns 6 percent, based on current market prices. Other companies with the same risk profile provide similar returns. KAO uses its weighted average cost of capital as its required rate of return. Calculate KAO's required rate of return.

2. A three-year investment project has the following estimated data: sales price = $65 per unit, variable costs = $33 per unit, fixed costs (excluding depreciation) = $4,000 per year, depreciation = $3,000 per year, required return = 10 percent, initial investment = $9,000, life = three years. Ignoring the effect of taxes, what is the accounting breakeven quantity? What is the economic breakeven quantity?

3. JMJ, Inc., is considering investing in one of three four-year investment alternatives. The estimated information about each alternative is included in the table below. Assume JMJ's required rate of return is 12 percent. Using the net present value technique, determine which of the three investments JMJ should select.

	Investment A	Investment B	Investment C
Cash Flow			
Initial Investment	−$30,000	−$30,000	−$30,000
Year 1	$20,000	$10,000	$15,000
Year 2	$20,000	$10,000	$12,000
Year 3		$12,000	$8,000
Year 4		$14,000	$8,000

4. Using the following information, calculate the internal rate of return for this project.

Initial Investment	Year 1 Cash Flow	Year 2 Cash Flow	Year 3 Cash Flow
$65,000	$26,000	$26,000	$26,000

5. CW Mutual Insurance is in an extremely competitive market for a specific line of business. The line of business is expected to have 100 percent of the loss paid at the end of the second year. CW management has set a target NPV for this line of business at $3,000. The initial premium estimate is $25,000, and policy expenses are expected to be 28 percent. The estimated present value of claims, assuming a 0 percent interest rate, is $15,000. Complete the following table, assuming no inflation, to determine the estimated gross premium required at each interest rate.

Interest Rate	PV of Claims	Target NPV	Required Investable Funds	Estimated Gross Premium
0%	$15,000	$3,000	$18,000	$25,000
2%		$3,000		
4%		$3,000		
6%		$3,000		
8%		$3,000		

Answers to Assignment 14 Questions

NOTE: These answers are provided to give students a basic understanding of acceptable types of responses. They often are not the only valid answers and are not intended to provide an exhaustive response to the questions.

Review Questions

1. The following process is used in making capital budgeting decisions:
    - Measuring the risk-adjusted profitability of each alternative
    - Ranking the alternatives according to their profitability
    - Choosing the one that provides the greatest profit potential

2. The following rates are used as the discount rate when making financial decisions:
    a. Investors—Use the required rate of return as the discount rate for any time-value-of-money calculations performed in making financial allocation decisions
    b. Companies—Use their weighted cost of capital as the discount rate in making allocation decisions

3. To calculate the weighted average cost of capital (WACC):

    (Cost of equity × Percentage equity) + (Cost of debt × Percentage debt).

4. Flotation costs are those associated with the issuance of new securities. They must be considered when making investment decisions. Although flotation costs do not increase the required rate of return on the investment, they do increase the amount of capital that must be raised to fund the project.

5. The following capital investment evaluation strategies are used to analyze investment alternatives:
    a. Accounting rate of return—Calculated by dividing the annual net income by the average annual investment in a project. This figure should be compared with the required rate of return, or to a standard selected by management, to determine whether to undertake a project.
    b. Payback rule—Payback is the length of time it takes for cumulative cash flows from a project to equal the original investment without taking account of the time value of money. The payback period is compared with a standard that is set by the company, and the project is accepted if it is less than or equal to the standard.
    c. Breakeven analysis—Determines the annual sales level at which the income from the project equals the costs of the project, as reported in the accounting records. Calculated as follows:

        Breakeven sales = Fixed costs (including depreciation) ÷ Profit percentage per sales dollar.

6. The major flaw in using the accounting rate of return in assessing capital investment is that it incorrectly weights revenues and costs because it ignores the time value of money. Distant cash flows receive the same weight as early flows, yet they are not equal.

7. The following costs are used in capital investment breakeven analysis:
    a. Fixed costs—Costs that remain constant over a range of sales, such as depreciation, insurance, rent, and administrative salaries

b. Profit per sales dollar—Equal to the sales price per unit less variable costs
c. Variable costs—Costs that are paid only when a sale occurs, such as the cost of material, costs of labor, and sales commissions

8. A project that breaks even on an accounting basis can pay for its own fixed operating expenses but does not provide for the return of the original investment or any compensation for the use of the capital invested.

   Economic breakeven is used to determine the minimum sales level needed to cover all the costs of an investment, including both the cost of capital and the return of capital. The cost of equipment is included in the amount of the original investment rather than being allocated over the investment's useful life; therefore, depreciation is excluded from the fixed costs. This formula provides a more accurate determination of payback period than the accounting breakeven formula.

9. The following cash flow techniques are used to analyze investment alternatives:
   a. Net present value (NPV)—The current value of expected future net cash flows. The NPV rule indicates that a company should accept all independent projects whose NPV is greater than zero—or, if two projects are mutually exclusive, the one with the higher NPV. Calculated as follows:

   $$NPV = -C_0 + (C_1 \div (1 + r)^1) + (C_2 \div (1 + r)^2) + (C_3 \div (1 + r)^3) + \ldots + (C_n \div (1 + r)^n).$$

   b. Internal rate of return (IRR)—Percentage rate of return on invested funds that produces a net present value of zero. The IRR rule states that a company should accept those investment projects whose expected internal rate of return is greater than the cost of capital. Calculated as follows:

   $$-C_0 + (C_1 \div (1 + r)^1) + (C_2 \div (1 + r)^2) + (C_3 \div (1 + r)^3) + \ldots + (C_n \div (1 + r)^n) = 0.$$

10. A lending project is one in which investment dollars are paid in one period and income is received in subsequent periods. A borrowing project is one in which money is received in one period and repaid in subsequent periods.

11. The following situations could lead to ambiguous decisions regarding investment decisions using NPV and IRR rules:
    - Lending projects compared with borrowing projects—When a company borrows, it should do so at an IRR that is less than the rate that must be paid for capital from alternative sources, generally choosing borrowing projects with a low IRR. If the NPV rule is used, the need to distinguish between borrowing and lending projects does not arise.
    - Multiple rates of return—These are present when the cash flows of the projects alternate from positive to negative cash flow more than once during the term of the project. Because IRR is the rate of return at which the NPV of the investment is zero, each time the cash flow changes, a new IRR is created. This makes the IRR rule difficult to apply. The NPV rule should be used in this instance.
    - Mutually exclusive projects—Differences in the scale or cash flow pattern of the projects can lead to ambiguous decisions. The company should estimate its cost of capital and then choose the project with the higher NPV since the NPV of a project represents the change in the company's net worth.

12. The following are two forms of capital rationing that may be used to limit a company's capital expenditures:
    (1) Soft rationing—A way for management to control spending and to focus on the projects that are most likely to create the greatest increase in shareholder wealth. Soft rationing is accomplished by setting specific limits on the amounts of capital available for investment or by increasing the cost of capital to be used as the discount rate for *NPV* and *IRR* calculations.
    (2) Hard rationing—The limitation of capital available for investment as a result of external constraints.
13. A company may have difficulty raising capital for the following reasons:
    - The company is under financial distress.
    - The credit environment is difficult.
    - The company does not yet have a track record.
14. An insurance contract follows the cash flow pattern of a borrowing project because the insurer receives the gross premium (less production and other expenses) and subsequently pays claims from these funds.
15. As the discount rate increases, an insurance policy adds more value to the insurer. The value increase for an insurance policy is derived from the spread between the discount rate and the inflation rate. The greater the spread, the higher the value added.
16. An insurer might use capital budgeting to identify the effects that writing, or reducing, lines of business will have on the company's value.
17. An insurer uses underwriting and net investment income in making capital budgeting decisions to determine underwriting profit margins in insurance rates.
18. Competition affects an insurer's investment income because it forces the insurer to pay market prices for investment assets. It affects an insurer's underwriting profits because the insurer needs to charge the market price for its policies to stay in business.

Application Questions

1. KAO's required return, its weighted average cost of capital, is calculated as follows:
   WACC = (Cost of equity × Percentage equity) + (Cost of debt × Percentage debt)
   Percentage equity = Equity ÷ Total capital
   Percentage debt = Debt ÷ Total capital
   WACC = [0.12 × ($1,000,000 ÷ $2,500,000)] + [0.06 × ($1,500,000 ÷ $2,500,000)]
   WACC = (0.12 × 0.4) + (0.06 × 0.6)
   WACC = 0.048 + 0.036
   WACC = 0.084, or 8.4%.

2. The accounting breakeven is calculated as follows:
    Breakeven quantity = Breakeven sales ÷ Price per unit
    Breakeven sales = (Fixed costs + Depreciation) ÷ Profit percentage per sales dollar
    Profit percentage per sales dollar = (Price − Variable costs) ÷ Price
    Profit percentage per sales dollar = ($65 − $33) ÷ $65 = 0.49 or 49%
    Breakeven sales = ($4,000 + $3,000) ÷ 0.49
    Breakeven sales = $14,286
    Breakeven quantity = $14,286 ÷ $65 = 220 units (219.78 rounded up).

    The economic breakeven, which includes operating cash flow (OCF) to repay the capital investment plus the required rate of return, is calculated as follows:
    Breakeven quantity = Breakeven sales ÷ Price per unit
    Breakeven sales = (Fixed costs + OCF) ÷ Profit percentage per sales dollar
    OCF = Investment ÷ PVA factor for three years at 10% [Present Value of an Annuity of $1 Per Period for n Periods, Table provided on National Exam]
    OCF = $9,000 ÷ 2.4869
    OCF = $3,618.96
    Breakeven sales = ($4,000 + $3,618.96) ÷ 0.49
    Breakeven sales = $15,548.90
    Breakeven quantity = $15,548.90 ÷ $65 = 240 units (239.22 rounded up).

3. Using the net present value technique, at a 12 percent required rate of return, JMJ should select Investment B. Although all investments are estimated to result in a positive net present value, Investment B results in the highest net present value of the three alternatives.

    This answer can be arrived at using three different methods:
    a. The present value tables provided on the exam
    b. A financial calculator
    c. The formula

    a. Using the Present Value tables

Present Value	Investment A	Investment B	Investment C
Initial Investment	−$30,000	−$30,000	−$30,000
PV of Year 1 CF PVF(n=1, i=12%) = 0.8929	$17,858	$8,929	$13,394
PV of Year 2 CF PVF(n=2, i=12%) = 0.7972	$15,944	$7,972	$9,566
PV of Year 3 CF PVF(n=3, i=12%) = 0.7118	0	$8,542	$5,694
PV of Year 4 CF PVF(n=3, i=12%) = 0.6355	0	$8,897	$5,084
Net present value	$3,802	$4,340	$3,738
Net Present Value = Initial Investment + sum of the present values of the cash flows			

b. Using a financial calculator

To solve for a net present value when cash flows are equal (Investment A), calculate the present value of the future cash flows (present value of an ordinary annuity) and subtract the initial investment.

Net present value = PV of future cash flows − initial investment

Investment A:

Values:

FV = 0

PMT = 20,000.00

I/Y = 12

N = 2

CPT − PV = -33,801 (Present value is shown as a negative number to represent how much you would have to invest today (cash outflow) to receive the 20,000 per year for the next 2 years to earn 12%).

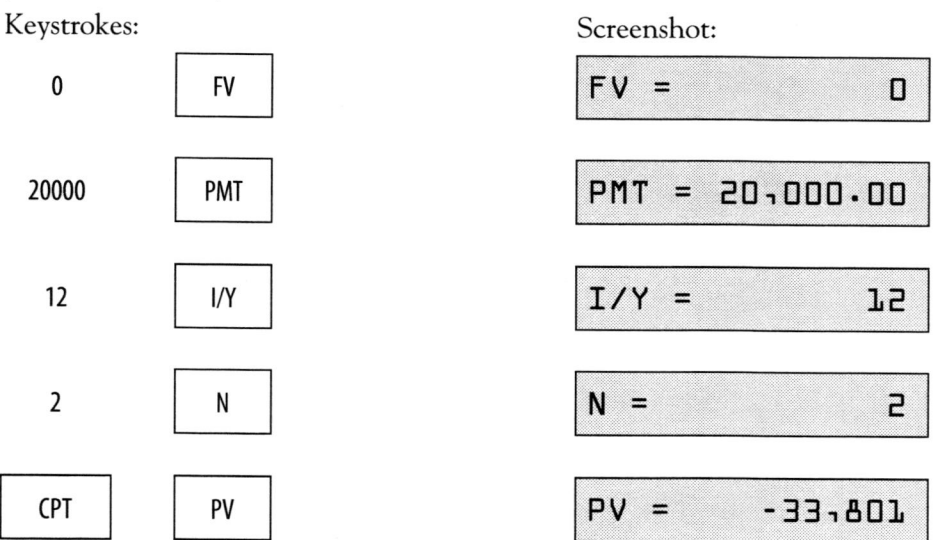

Keystrokes:

Input	Key	Screenshot
0	FV	FV = 0
20000	PMT	PMT = 20,000.00
12	I/Y	I/Y = 12
2	N	N = 2
CPT	PV	PV = -33,801

Net Present Value = 33,801 − 30,000 = $3,801 Note that the present value of future cash flows here is not shown as a negative. The investment's initial investment of 30,000 is shown as the negative because that is how much you are investing to generate the 20,000 cash flows for the next two years.

To solve for the net present value when cash flows are unequal, use the cash flow worksheet as shown below.

Investment B:

Keystrokes:

			Screenshot:
	CF		CFo = 0.00
30000	+/-	Enter	CFo = -30,000.00
	↓		C01 = 0.00
10000	Enter		C01 = 10,000.00
	↓		F01 = 1.00
	↓		C02 = 0.00
10000	Enter		C02 = 10,000.00
	↓		F02 = 1.00
	↓		C03 = 0.00
12000	Enter		C03 = 12,000.00
	↓		F03 = 1.00
	↓		C04 = 0.00
14000	Enter		C04 = 14,000.00
	↓		F04 = 1.00
	NPV		I = 0.00
12	Enter		I = 12.00
	↓		NPV = 0.00
	CPT		NPV = 4,339.13

The same process can be used to solve for Investment C.

c. Using the formula

$$NPV = -C_0 + (C_1 \div (1+r)^t) + (C_2 \div (1+r)^t) + (C_3 \div (1+r)^t) + \ldots + (C_n \div (1+r)^n),$$

where:

C_0 = Cash flow at beginning of project,
C_t = Payment at year t for t = 1, through $t = n$,
r = Discount rate,
n = Number of payments, and
t = Year in which payment is made.

Investment A:
NPV = -30,000 +(20,000/(1+.12)¹) +(20,000/(1+.12)²)
NPV = -30,000 +(20,000/1.12) + (20,000/1.2544)
NPV = -30,000 +17,857.14 + 15,943.88
NPV = -30,000 + 33,802.02
NPV = 3,802.02

Investment B:
NPV = -30,000 +(10,000/(1+.12)¹) +(10,000/(1+.12)²) +(12,000/(1+.12)³) +(14,000/(1+.12)⁴)
NPV = -30,000 +(10,000/1.12) + (10,000/1.2544) +(12,000/1.4049) +(14,000/1.5735)
NPV = -30,000 +8928.57 + 7971.94 + 8541.53 + 8897.36
NPV = -30,000 + 34,339.40
NPV = 4,339.40

Investment B:
NPV = -30,000 +(15,000/(1+.12)¹) +(12,000/(1+.12)²) +(8,000/(1+.12)³) +(8,000/(1+.12)⁴)
NPV = -30,000 +(15,000/1.12) + (12,000/1.2544) +(8,000/1.4049) +(8,000/1.5735)
NPV = -30,000 +13392.86 + 9566.33 + 5694.36 + 5084.21
NPV = -30,000 + 33737.76
NPV = 3,737.76

4. Using the following information, the internal rate of return for the project is 9.7 percent. This answer can be reached using a financial calculator or by the trial and error method.

   a. Using a Financial Calculator:

   Values:

   PV = -65,000

   FV = 0

   PMT = 26,000

   N = 3

   CPT – I/Y = 9.7

   Keystrokes:

   Screenshot:

   65000 [+/-] [PV] → PV = −65,000

   0 [FV] → FV = 0

   26000 [PMT] → PMT = 26,000

   3 [N] → N = 3

   [CPT] [I/Y] → I/Y = 9.7

   b. Trial and Error

Initial investment	Year 1 Cash Flow	Year 2 Cash Flow	Year 3 Cash Flow
$65,000	$26,000	$26,000	$26,000

   Without a financial calculator, the *IRR* is found by trial and error as follows. The *IRR* is the rate at which the *NPV* of the project is 0. An initial interest rate is selected, the *NPV* is calculated, the rate is then adjusted to find a new *NPV*, and this process is repeated until the *NPV* is zero.

PV @ 9% Initial Investment	PV @ 9% Year 1 Cash Flow	PV @ 9% Year 2 Cash Flow	PV @ 9% Year 3 Cash Flow	PV @ 9%
$65,000	$23,853	$21,884	$20,777	$814

PV @ 10% Initial Investment	PV @ 10% Year 1 Cash Flow	PV @ 10% Year 2 Cash Flow	PV @ 10% Year 3 Cash Flow	PV @ 10%
$65,000	$23,636	$21,488	$19,534	−$342

Interpolation can be used to determine a close estimate of the *IRR*. The difference between the *NPV* at 9 percent and at 10 percent is $1,156 ($814 + $342). Therefore, the *IRR* must be 9 percent plus the portion of the 1 percent difference between 9 percent and 10 percent that decreases the *NPV* by $814. This is calculated as follows: 1% × ($814 ÷ $1,156) = 0.7%. Therefore, the *IRR* is 9.7 percent.

5.

Interest Rate (1)	PV of Claims (2) Discount two years using (1)	Target NPV (3)	Required Investable Funds (4) = (3) + (2)	Estimated Gross Premium (5) = (4) ÷ 0.72
0%	$15,000	$3,000	$18,000	$25,000
2%	$14,417 = 15,000 *PVF (n=2,%i = 2%)	$3,000	$17,417	$24,190
4%	$13,868 = 15,000 *PVF (n=2,%i = 4%)	$3,000	$16,868	$23,428
6%	$13,350 = 15,000 *PVF (n=2,%i = 6%)	$3,000	$16,350	$22,708
8%	$12,860 = 15,000 *PVF (n=2,%i = 8%)	$3,000	$15,860	$22,028

Direct Your Learning

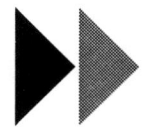

Mergers and Acquisitions

Educational Objectives

After learning the content of this assignment, you should be able to:

1. Describe the typical ways in which a change in business ownership or control can be accomplished.
2. Describe the reasons for acquisitions.
3. Explain how gains and costs from acquisitions are determined.
4. Explain why the following must be considered before any acquisition decisions are made: due diligence, tax aspects, financial aspects, and financial statement effects.
5. Explain the various defenses a company can use to prevent a takeover.
6. Explain why the owners of selling companies generally gain more than the owners of acquiring companies.

ASSIGNMENT 15

Study Materials

Required Reading:
- Finance for Risk Management and Insurance Professionals
  - Chapter 15

Study Aids:
- SMART Online Practice Exams
- SMART Study Aids
  - Review Notes and Flash Cards—Assignment 15

Outline

- **Changes in Ownership and Control**
- **Reasons for Acquisitions**
    - A. Cost Savings
        1. Efficiencies
        2. Tax Advantages
        3. Reduced Cost of Financial Distress
    - B. Synergies
    - C. Competitive Advantage
    - D. Increased Earnings per Share
    - E. Management Interests
    - F. Use of Excess Funds
- **Acquisition Gains and Costs**
- **Mechanics of Acquisitions**
    - A. Due Diligence
    - B. Tax Aspects
    - C. Financial Aspects
    - D. Financial Statement Effects
    - E. Takeover Defenses
- **Financial Results of Acquisitions**
- **Acquisitions in the Property-Casualty Insurance Industry**
- **Summary**

study tips: Studying before sleeping helps you retain material better than studying before undertaking other tasks.

Key Words and Phrases

Define or describe each of the words and phrases listed below.

Merger (p. 15.4)

Acquisition (p. 15.4)

Consolidation (p. 15.4)

Takeover (p. 15.4)

Proxy contest (p. 15.4)

Tender offer (p. 15.5)

Divestiture (p. 15.5)

Spin-off (p. 15.5)

Horizontal acquisition (p. 15.6)

Vertical acquisition (p. 15.6)

Conglomerate acquisition (p. 15.6)

Revenue efficiency (p. 15.6)

Cost efficiency (p. 15.6)

Due diligence (p. 15.15)

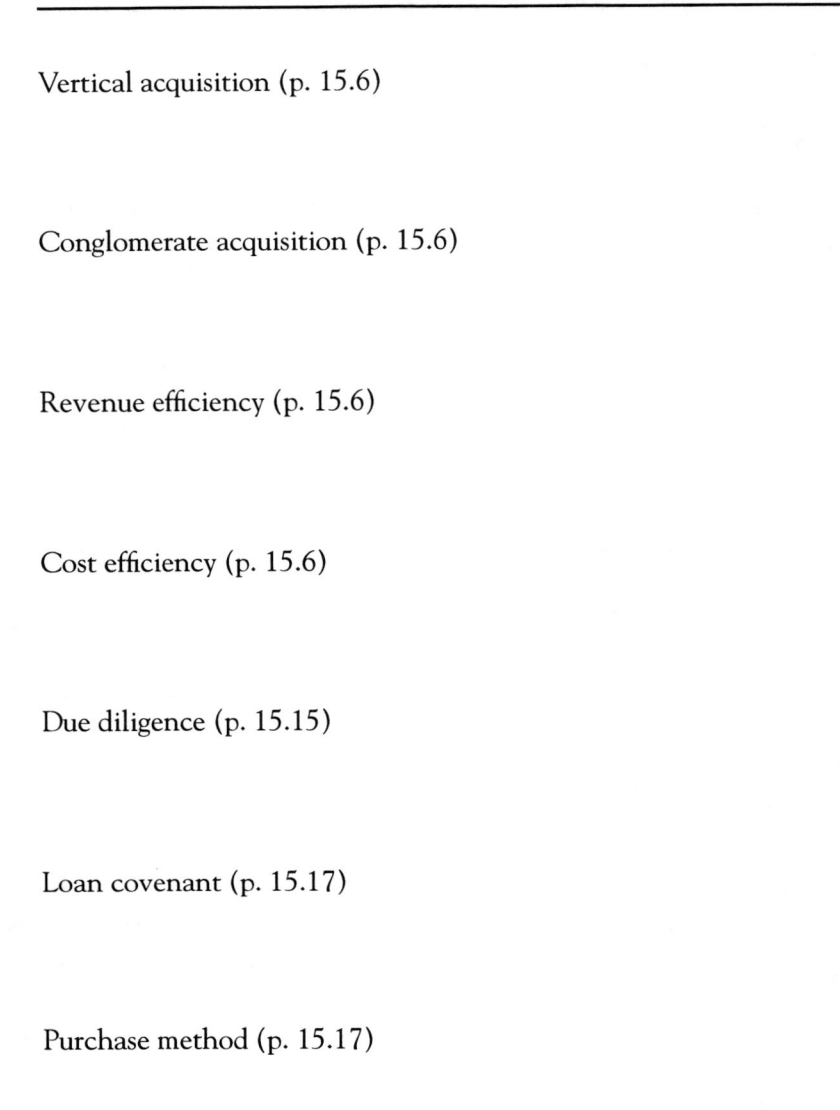

Loan covenant (p. 15.17)

Purchase method (p. 15.17)

Review Questions

1. Identify market conditions that may lead to corporate changes in companies. (p. 15.3)

2. Describe how change in ownership and control of a company is accomplished through the following:
   a. Merger (p. 15.4)

   b. Acquisition (p. 15.4)

   c. Consolidation (p. 15.4)

   d. Takeover (p. 15.4)

   e. Proxy contest (p. 15.4)

   f. Tender offer (p. 15.5)

g. Divestiture (p. 15.5)

h. Spin-off (p. 15.5)

3. Describe how the following types of acquisitions differ:
   a. Horizontal acquisition (p. 15.6)

   b. Vertical acquisition (p. 15.6)

   c. Conglomerate acquisition (p. 15.6)

4. List the possible reasons for acquisitions. (p. 15.6)

5. Explain the ways an acquisition can lead to cost savings for a company. (pp. 15.6–15.8)

6. Describe how a company can achieve revenue and cost efficiencies. (pp. 15.6–15.7)

7. Explain how companies can experience cost savings from acquisitions due to economies of scale and economies of scope. (p. 15.9)

8. Describe how a company's competitive advantage in the marketplace might be improved through a horizontal acquisition. (p. 15.10)

9. Describe an indication that an acquisition resulted in economic gain and how the value of a gain is determined. (p. 15.12)

10. Explain how the market price is established regarding a publicly traded company and a privately held company. (p. 15.13)

11. Explain how to ensure that the gains to both parties are equal in an acquisition, regardless of whether it is financed with cash or with stocks. (p. 15.14)

12. Describe the advantages and disadvantages of acquisitions as a way to change ownership or control of a company. (p. 15.15)

13. Describe the purpose of due diligence during an acquisition. (p. 15.15)

14. Identify areas of financial concern when performing due diligence in the insurance industry. (p. 15.17)

15. Define how goodwill arises under the purchase method of accounting for an acquisition. (p. 15.17)

16. Explain why a buyer might be willing to pay more than the market value of a target company's net worth. (p. 15.17)

17. Describe how the following levels of ownership interest affect financial statements under GAAP: (p. 15.18)
    - Ownership interests of more than 50 percent

    - Ownership interests between 20 percent and 50 percent

    - Ownership interests of less than 20 percent

18. Describe defensive tactics a firm might use to make a takeover less likely. (p. 15.19)

19. List the common defensive tactics collectively known as "shark repellents" used to prevent a takeover. (pp. 15.19–15.20)

20. Explain why target companies in an acquisition generally earn higher percentage returns than acquiring companies. (p. 15.20)

Application Questions

1. ABC Company has offered $510 million cash for all of the common stock in XYZ Corporation. Based on recent market information, XYZ is worth $380 million as an independent operation. If the merger makes economic sense for ABC, what is the minimum estimated value of the synergistic benefits (goodwill) from the merger?

GOODWILL = PURCHASE PRICE − NET FAIR MARKET VALUE

$510 MILLION − $380 MILLION = $130 MILLION

2. ABC Company's shareholders have voted in favor of accepting a buyout offer from XYZ Corporation. Information about each firm is as follows:

	ABC	XYZ
Price-earnings ratio	5.25	21
Shares outstanding	60,000	180,000
Earnings	$300,000	$675,000

ABC shareholders will receive one share of XYZ stock for every three shares that they hold in ABC.

60,000 ÷ 3 = 20,000 NEW SHARES ISSUED TO TARGET

a. What will XYZ's earnings per share (EPS) be after the acquisition?

POST ACQUISITION EPS = (BUYERS NET INCOME + TARGET NET INCOME) / (EXISTING BUYER'S SHARES OUTSTANDING + NEW SHARES ISSUED TO TARGET)

= (675,000 + 300,000) ÷ (180,000 + 20,000)
= 975,000 ÷ 200,000
= 4.875

b. What will the post-acquisition price-earnings (PE) ratio be, if the acquisition's NPV is zero?

SHARE PRICE = (NI * PE) ÷ SHARES OUTSTANDING
= (675,000 * 21) ÷ 180,000
= 78.75

PE RATIO = SHARE PRICE ÷ EPS
= 78.75 ÷ $4.875
= $16.15

Answers to Assignment 15 Questions

NOTE: These answers are provided to give students a basic understanding of acceptable types of responses. They often are not the only valid answers and are not intended to provide an exhaustive response to the questions.

Review Questions

1. Market conditions that may lead to corporate changes in companies include deregulation, technological innovation, and capital market transformations.

2. Change in ownership and control of a company may be accomplished through the following:
   a. Merger—Two or more business entities are combined into one. Assets and liabilities of the two companies are merged, and the target ceases to exist as a separate entity.
   b. Acquisition—The purchase of one company's stock by another company. The buyer continues to exist, and the target can also continue to exist.
   c. Consolidation—The combination of two or more business entities into a new entity. Both the buyer and the target cease to exist, and a new combined entity is formed.
   d. Takeover—Change in the control of a company, either friendly or hostile.
   e. Proxy contest—A takeover is achieved by obtaining the voting rights of the target's shareholders. May be used to facilitate an acquisition so that the buyer avoids paying a premium for the target.
   f. Tender offer—Purchase offer made directly to the shareholders of the target, typically at an offer price greater than the current market price. It is usually contingent on the buyer's obtaining a minimum of 80 percent of the target company's voting shares to avoid income taxes.
   g. Divestiture—Disposal or sale of part of a company. The selling company gives up all ownership in the divested portion.
   h. Spin-off—Creation of a new company from part of an existing company. Shareholders of the existing company typically receive shares in the new company in the same proportion as their ownership in the original company.

3. Acquisitions differ according to whether or not the buyer and the target operate in the same business area:
   a. Horizontal acquisition—Companies are in the same line of business.
   b. Vertical acquisition—Companies are involved in related lines of business but at different stages of production.
   c. Conglomerate acquisition—Companies are in unrelated lines of business.

4. The following are possible reasons for acquisitions:
   - Cost savings
   - Synergies
   - Competitive advantage
   - Increased earnings per share
   - Management interests
   - Use of excess funds

5. An acquisition can lead to cost savings for a company in the following ways:
   - Efficiencies—Acquisitions may lead to more efficient use of a company's financial resources by way of revenue efficiencies or cost efficiencies.
   - Tax advantages—Efficiency can be achieved by reducing income taxes through increasing the level of debt, increasing cash flows from recovery of taxes, and reducing income on which tax is calculated through the treatment of depreciable assets.
   - Reduced cost of financial distress—Debt holders and creditors reduce their credit risk because the debt risk of the combined company is lower, and the value of limited liability is lower when debt holders have reduced risk because they can claim against the combined cash flows.

6. A company achieves revenue efficiency when its revenues cannot be increased, holding economic inputs constant, by combining the company with another entity or entities.

   A company achieves cost efficiency when its costs cannot be decreased, holding economic outputs constant, by combining the company with another entity or entities.

7. Savings from economies of scale are expected in horizontal acquisitions and are size driven, leaving the range of products and services unchanged. If one or both companies have excess capacity that will be more fully used when the two companies combine, then reduced capital needs and associated capital costs will result.

   Savings from economies of scope are expected in vertical acquisitions and result from broadening the range of products and services offered. Cost savings can come from the use of shared resources, improvements in a company's competitive position, and additional revenue opportunities.

8. A company's competitive advantage in the marketplace might be improved through a horizontal acquisition. When few companies compete in a line of business or market, acquisitions are likely to increase the market power of the combined company, which enables the company to influence price, product offerings, and contract terms.

9. One indication that an acquisition resulted in economic gain is if the companies combined are more valuable together than apart, demonstrated by additional net cash inflows. The value of the economic gain is calculated as follows:

$$G = V_{AB} - (V_A + V_B).$$

10. The market price of a publicly traded company is directly observable. The market price of a privately held company is estimated using valuation techniques, such as a discounted cash flow valuation model. In an acquisition financed with cash, the acquisition price is simply the amount of cash paid for the target firm. The acquisition price in a stock acquisition depends on the market price per share of stock in the combined entity after the merger.

11. To ensure that the gains to both parties are equal in an acquisition, the number of shares issued in an acquisition financed with stock must reflect the benefits of the acquisition by using the expected share price once the acquisition has been completed.

12. The advantages of acquisitions as a way to change ownership or control of a company include simplicity, lower costs, and no need to transfer title to individual assets or assume individual liabilities. A disadvantage is that acquisitions must be approved by a majority of shareholders of both companies.

13. Due diligence performed during an acquisition provides a foundation for valuation analysis, deal negotiation, and the post-acquisition integration process. The due diligence process covers a wide range of business areas.

14. An area of financial concern when performing due diligence in the insurance industry is the solvency position of an insurer. The buyer also needs to ascertain whether existing agreements impose any potential restrictions on financial operations.

15. Goodwill arises under the purchase method of accounting when the purchase price exceeds the estimated fair market value of the net worth.

16. A buyer might be willing to pay more than the market value of the target company's net worth because the acquired company may have franchise value related to a brand name, expertise (human assets), technology, or other sources of competitive advantage beyond the fair value of the tangible and intangible assets recorded in its financial statements.

17. Levels of acquisition ownership interest have the following effects on financial statements under GAAP:
    - Ownership interests of more than 50 percent—The target company must consolidate the results of the target into its financial statements using the purchase method.
    - Ownership interests between 20 percent and 50 percent—The investment in the target firm is recorded as an asset on the buyer's balance sheet. This investment account is increased for the acquiring company's share of net income of the target and decreased for any dividends and returns of capital received using the equity method of accounting.
    - Ownership interests of less than 20 percent—Recorded at cost on the buyer's financial statements but might be adjusted for changes in market value under fair value accounting rules.

18. A firm (target) can make a takeover less likely by employing defensive tactics designed to thwart unfriendly takeovers, such as the following:
    - Initiate a target repurchase from a raider in order to terminate the takeover attempt
    - Find a friendly buyer, known as a white knight
    - Make the acquisition more difficult or costly to the bidder by using "shark repellents"

19. The following defensive tactics, collectively known as "shark repellents," are used to prevent a takeover:
    - Golden parachute
    - Super majority
    - Staggered board
    - Poison pills
    - Poison puts
    - Crown jewel
    - Lockup

20. Target companies generally earn higher percentage returns in an acquisition transaction than acquiring companies because acquiring companies are typically larger. Therefore, on a percentage basis, the acquisition benefits do not increase the buyer's value as significantly as the target's.

Application Questions

1. The minimum estimated value of the synergistic benefits (goodwill) from the merger is $130 million, calculated as follows:

    Goodwill = Purchase price − Net fair market value

    = $510 million − $380 million

    = $130 million.

2. After the ABC acquisition:
    a. XYZ's earnings per share (EPS) will be $4.875, calculated as follows:

        Post-acquisition EPS = (Buyer's Net income + Target Net income) ÷ (Existing buyer shares outstanding + New shares issued to target)

        = ($675,000 + $300,000) ÷ (180,000 + 20,000*)

        = $975,000 ÷ 200,000

        = $4.875.

    *ABC shareholders will receive, in total, 20,000 shares = 60,000 ÷ 3.

    b. Because the transaction's *NPV* is zero, it can be assumed that the price after the merger is the same as before the acquisition, $78.75 per share, calculated as follows:

        Share price = (NI × PE) ÷ Shares outstanding

        = ($675,000 × 21) ÷ 180,000

        = $78.75.

    Therefore, the post-acquisition price-earnings (PE) ratio is 16.15, calculated as follows:

    PE = Share price ÷ EPS

    = $78.75 ÷ $4.875

    = 16.15.

Exam Information

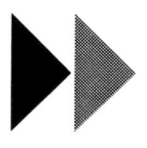

About Institute Exams

Exam questions are based on the Educational Objectives stated in the course guide and textbook. The exam is designed to measure whether you have met those Educational Objectives. The exam does not test every Educational Objective. Instead, it tests over a balanced sample of Educational Objectives.

How to Prepare for Institute Exams

What can you do to prepare for an Institute exam? Students who pass Institute exams do the following:

- Use the assigned study materials. Focus your study on the Educational Objectives presented at the beginning of each course guide assignment. Thoroughly read the textbook and any other assigned materials, and then complete the course guide exercises. Choose a study method that best suits your needs; for example, participate in a traditional class, online class, or informal study group; or study on your own. Use the Institutes' SMART Study Aids (if available) for practice and review. If this course has an associated SMART Online Practice Exams product, you will find an access code on the inside back cover of this course guide. This access code allows you to print (in PDF format) a full practice exam and to take additional online practice exams that will simulate an actual credentialing exam.

- Become familiar with the types of test questions asked on the exam. The practice exam in this course guide or in the SMART Online Practice Exams product will help you understand the different types of questions you will encounter on the exam.

- Maximize your test-taking time. Successful students use the sample exam in the course guide or in the SMART Online Practice Exams product to practice pacing themselves. Learning how to manage your time during the exam ensures that you will complete all of the test questions in the time allotted.

Types of Exam Questions

The exam for this course consists of objective questions of several types.

The Correct-Answer Type

In this type of question, the question stem is followed by four responses, one of which is absolutely correct. Select the *correct* answer.

> Which one of the following persons evaluates requests for insurance to determine which applicants are accepted and which are rejected?
>
> a. The premium auditor
>
> b. The loss control representative
>
> c. The underwriter
>
> d. The risk manager

The Best-Answer Type

In this type of question, the question stem is followed by four responses, only one of which is best, given the statement made or facts provided in the stem. Select the *best* answer.

> Several people within an insurer might be involved in determining whether an applicant for insurance is accepted. Which one of the following positions is primarily responsible for determining whether an applicant for insurance is accepted?
>
> a. The loss control representative
>
> b. The customer service representative
>
> c. The underwriter
>
> d. The premium auditor

The Incomplete-Statement or Sentence-Completion Type

In this type of question, the last part of the question stem consists of a portion of a statement rather than a direct question. Select the phrase that *correctly* or *best* completes the sentence.

> Residual market plans designed for individuals who are unable to obtain insurance on their personal property in the voluntary market are called
>
> a. VIN plans.
> b. Self-insured retention plans.
> c. Premium discount plans.
> d. FAIR plans.

"All of the Above" Type

In this type of question, only one of the first three answers could be correct, or all three might be correct, in which case the best answer would be "All of the above." Read all the answers and select the *best* answer.

> When a large commercial insured's policy is up for renewal, who is likely to provide input to the renewal decision process?
>
> a. The underwriter
> b. The loss control representative
> c. The producer
> d. All of the above

"All of the following, EXCEPT:" Type

In this type of question, responses include three correct answers and one answer that is incorrect or is clearly the least correct. Select the *incorrect* or *least correct* answer.

> All of the following adjust insurance claims, EXCEPT:
>
> a. Insurer claim representatives
> b. Premium auditors
> c. Producers
> d. Independent adjusters

About the Code of Professional Ethics

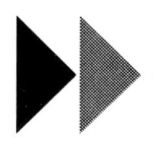

This is a brief summary of information appearing in greater detail in the Code of Professional Ethics, which is among the CPCU 510 study materials.

All CPCU candidates and CPCUs are bound by the Code of Professional Ethics of the American Institute for CPCU. The Code describes both high goals and minimum standards of conduct.

1. The high goals described in the Canons challenge all CPCUs and CPCU candidates to aspire to the highest level of ethical performance in all of their professional activities.
2. The minimum standards of conduct, described in the Rules, maintain the integrity of the CPCU designation. CPCUs and CPCU candidates are obligated to at least meet the minimum standards in the Rules, and failure to do so may subject a CPCU—or a CPCU candidate—to disciplinary measures.

CPCU candidates study the Code and are tested in CPCU 510 to ensure that all CPCUs understand their ethical obligations. The ultimate goal of the Code is to foster highly ethical conduct on the part of all CPCUs.

The Canons and Rules of the Code of Professional Ethics

Canon 1—CPCUs should endeavor at all times to place the public interest above their own.

Rule R1.1—A CPCU has a duty to understand and abide by all *Rules* of conduct which are prescribed in the *Code of Professional Ethics of the American Institute*.

Rule R1.2—A CPCU shall not advocate, sanction, participate in, cause to be accomplished, otherwise carry out through another, or condone any act which the CPCU is prohibited from performing by the *Rules* of this *Code*.

Canon 2—CPCUs should seek continually to maintain and improve their professional knowledge, skills, and competence.

Rule R2.1—A CPCU shall keep informed on those technical matters that are essential to the maintenance of the CPCU's professional competence in insurance, risk management, or related fields.

Canon 3—CPCUs should obey all laws and regulations, and should avoid any conduct or activity which would cause unjust harm to others.

Rule R3.1—In the conduct of business or professional activities, a CPCU shall not engage in any act or omission of a dishonest, deceitful, or fraudulent nature.

Rule R3.2—A CPCU shall not allow the pursuit of financial gain or other personal benefit to interfere with the exercise of sound professional judgment and skills.

Rule R3.3—A CPCU shall not violate any law or regulation relating to professional activities or commit any felony.

Canon 4—CPCUs should be diligent in the performance of their occupational duties and should continually strive to improve the functioning of the insurance mechanism.

Rule R4.1—A CPCU shall competently and consistently discharge his or her occupational duties.

Rule R4.2—A CPCU shall support efforts to effect such improvements in claims settlement, contract design, investment, marketing, pricing, reinsurance, safety engineering, underwriting, and other insurance operations as will both inure to the benefit of the public and improve the overall efficiency with which the insurance mechanism functions.

Canon 5—CPCUs should assist in maintaining and raising professional standards in the insurance business.

Rule R5.1—A CPCU shall support personnel policies and practices which will attract qualified individuals to the insurance business, provide them with ample and equal opportunities for advancement, and encourage them to aspire to the highest levels of professional competence and achievement.

Rule R5.2—A CPCU shall encourage and assist qualified individuals who wish to pursue CPCU or other studies which will enhance their professional competence.

Rule R5.3—A CPCU shall support the development, improvement, and enforcement of such laws, regulations, and codes as will foster competence and ethical conduct on the part of all insurance practitioners and inure to the benefit of the public.

Rule R5.4—A CPCU shall not withhold information or assistance officially requested by appropriate regulatory authorities who are investigating or prosecuting any alleged violation of the laws or regulations governing the qualifications or conduct of insurance practitioners.

Canon 6—CPCUs should strive to establish and maintain dignified and honorable relationships with those whom they serve, with fellow insurance practitioners, and with members of other professions.

Rule R6.1—A CPCU shall keep informed on the legal limitations imposed upon the scope of his or her professional activities.

Rule R6.2—A CPCU shall not disclose to another person any confidential information entrusted to, or obtained by, the CPCU in the course of the CPCU's business or professional activities, unless a disclosure of such information is required by law or is made to a person who necessarily must have the information in order to discharge legitimate occupational or professional duties.

Rule R6.3—In rendering or proposing to render professional services for others, a CPCU shall not knowingly misrepresent or conceal any limitations on the CPCU's ability to provide the quantity or quality of professional services required by the circumstances.

Canon 7—CPCUs should assist in improving the public understanding of insurance and risk management.

Rule R7.1—A CPCU shall support efforts to provide members of the public with objective information concerning their risk management and insurance needs and the products, services, and techniques which are available to meet their needs.

Rule R7.2—A CPCU shall not misrepresent the benefits, costs, or limitations of any risk management technique or any product or service of an insurer.

Canon 8—CPCUs should honor the integrity of the CPCU designation and respect the limitations placed on its use.

Rule R8.1—A CPCU shall use the CPCU designation and the CPCU key only in accordance with the relevant *Guidelines* promulgated by the American Institute.

Rule R8.2—A CPCU shall not attribute to the mere possession of the designation depth or scope of knowledge, skills, and professional capabilities greater than those demonstrated by successful completion of the CPCU program.

Rule R8.3—A CPCU shall not make unfair comparisons between a person who holds the CPCU designation and one who does not.

Rule R8.4—A CPCU shall not write, speak, or act in such a way as to lead another to reasonably believe the CPCU is officially representing the American Institute, unless the CPCU has been duly authorized to do so by the American Institute.

Canon 9—CPCUs should assist in maintaining the integrity of the *Code of Professional Ethics*.

Rule R9.1—A CPCU shall not initiate or support the CPCU candidacy of any individual known by the CPCU to engage in business practices which violate the ethical standards prescribed by this *Code*.

Rule R9.2—A CPCU possessing unprivileged information concerning an alleged violation of this *Code* shall, upon request, reveal such information to the tribunal or other authority empowered by the American Institute to investigate or act upon the alleged violation.

Rule R9.3—A CPCU shall report promptly to the American Institute any information concerning the use of the CPCU designation by an unauthorized person.